CRAFT MANUAL

of

Northwest

INDIAN BEADING

by
GEORGE M. WHITE

Ronan, Montana

Copyright 1971 by
GEORGE M. WHITE

Tenth Printing, November, 1994

Illustrations and drawings by the author, with
the exception of those by C. M. Russell, which
are from the author's collection.

1

December 29, 1925

Dr. G M White

Brother I got your letter in regards to the Indian dress and am sending you some patterns these clothes could be made easy in tan colerd cloth that would look like skin the skirt if the animal was large enough like a buffalo cow ore an Elk was made of one peace leggons were always one skin the sides scolloped fringed or a plane flap some times the seemes of a shirt were fringed shirt legans and britch clout was the Indian dress over all was worn a blanket ore robe I hope these Sketches are what you want whishing you a happy New Year
Your Brother
C M Russell

The correspondence was in reference to the making of Indian costumes for the Lewistown, Montana Elks Band. Some forty-five members were dressed in Eagle headdresses and outfits designed from Russells sketches. The drum-major wore a full length bonnet at least five and a half feet long which required the feathers from five birds.

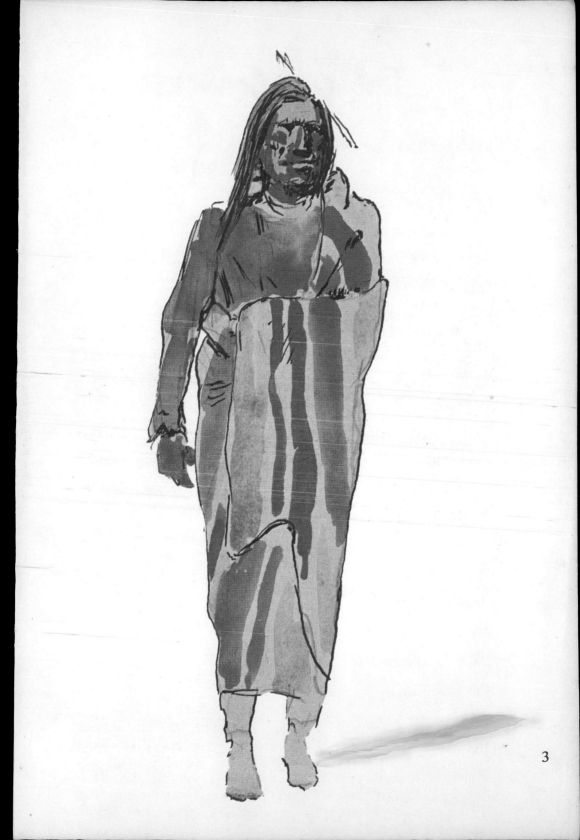

Table of Contents

INDEX OF COLOR PRINTS

Introduction

We might look at handcraft as a link in the chain of manipulative development that put man on the moon. This manipulative urge seems to be man's destiny: to mark, to change, to shape the world---or perhaps the universe.

Handcraft, as such, is a uniquely human activity of creativity and is nourished and sustained by social approval.

The development of certain handcraft results from man's universal urge to mark himself as well as his world. He seems compelled to attach things to himself, to mark his skin, pierce his nose, ears, lips and other parts of his body. In regions where clothing would cover his body markings, he marked his clothing.

The North American Indian, governed by the same universal urge as all men and by the same 'optical mechanics', took pleasure in decorating his world. The productivity of his hands and mind that has come to us through the ages is magnificent and overwhelming. This book, however, will focus on a limited group of people and a limited geographical area.

The North American continent was, by 1400 A. D., fairly well occupied by various groups of people. Their languages, customs, values and ideals were adequate for their way of life. Their economic system was sufficient to provide a degree of affluence which is the pre-requisite for handcraft.

Affluence, for our purpose, will refer to accumulative materials such as food, tools, weapons, household articles and so on. Their accumulative potential was low and a loss of a portion of their accumulative materials could cause great hardship.

An account of a Pend d'Oreille hunting party can well illustrate this. A large party was hunting in Eastern Montana and had the misfortune of being raided. A few people were killed, but the most severe blow to the total company was the loss of most of their horses. Being too far a-field for assistance from relatives in the Flathead Valley, they were forced to abandon most of their household materials, including tipis. Many men, children and women carrying babies on their backs, walked the full distance back to the Flathead Valley. Ten years later this group was still in an impoverished condition, partly from a general decline in ecomomics of the whole tribe, but also because of the time and energy required to accumulate household materials.

Foodstuffs were accumulative to limited degree, and a hard winter might cause suffering or starvation. But if the main body of accumulative materials were intact by spring, normal life would soon be resumed.

In general, affluence required a relief valve. Annual reunions of various bands of a tribe, or various ceremonies, could consume certain surplusses of food and enable an exchange of handcraft. These affairs were important events in the Indian life, but were surpassed by the excitement and anticipation of trading fairs with strange people.

The lack of an interpretor or verbal communication was neatly taken care of by sign language, as various groups exchanged their wares. Eye catching trinkets and numerous other hand-crafted articles changed hands. More than this, these people--highly skilled in seeing and reading the tiny details of their world--would take home with them a great deal of information about the strange people and their handcraft.

The master-craftsman could probably glean many ideas and techniques by merely examining an article. From the stimulus of such a meeting, the master-craftsman might reproduce a design or color combination which, if pleasing, might start a new trend that would be incorporated into the traditional handcraft.

A stone age culture demanded manual labor. The survival of the people was dependent on the productivity of the hands. Under these conditions, nearly every member of a group was skilled in performing some manual activity required by the group. The master-craftsman was one with special talents and intelligence--who, many times with artistic insight--created the ultimate piece of work.

Within the framework of Indian trade and trading fairs, many articles moved long distances from the place of their origin. Thus today, certain identifiable objects help determine some of these old Indian trade routes. Without doubt, handcraft of various sorts moved along these routes.

Handcraft in its fullest meaning would necessarily cover any object that has been marked or shaped by man. A proper study of the various types of handcraft can yield a wealth of information about the dynamics of the old Indian culture. We can see the flux and flow of people, their ability to change, to conquer adversity and to survive. We can see their ability to master new materials and tech-

9

niques.   Furthermore, we can see their intelligence and skills.

The introduction of European goods was beneficial to the Indian economy for the most part. The horse was quickly accepted, and a new way of life developed to accommodate the horse and the new affluance it provided. Metal tools quickly replaced those of stone. Guns replaced the bow and arrow. However, the introduction of the European economic system and its technology was at such a rapid rate that the Indian people could not adjust and retain their own economic integrity. This led to their degradation.

The earliest northern contacts were reportedly made in 1497, when fishing vessels, pushing upriver in search of suitable locations to dry and preserve cod fish, contacted Indian people. A casual exchange of gifts revealed the value of Indian furs. Cod fishing was soon forgotten in favor of more lucrative fur trading.

Various trading companies were chartered and private capital invested. The business world of that day was much the same as today, with its credit, bond, interest rate, cost, market, intrigue and so on. Economic pressures caused the rapid relentless drive into the interior. By 1850 most of the Indian people of North America had been in contact with European goods and people. In fact the Indian people of the eastern half of the continent had already begun their long economic depression.

Old Indian trade routes carried Western goods to interior people long before the trader reached them. Many displaced people of the eastern coastal areas who had lost their struggle with the white economic system drifted west, bringing bits of European goods into the interior.

Lewis and Clark papers report seeing large necklace trade beads in what is now Montana and Idaho in 1805-06. Ross Cox reported similar facts in 1812-13 along the upper Columbia River. He also mentioned that South Sea Islander deck hands were employed in up-river trading. These people could have introduced the cowrie shell which became a favorite object for dress decorations in the manner that elk teeth were used by Crow women.

He mentioned also that when a large amount of sewing thimbles were brought in, he was amazed to see that the women preferred them for dress decorations, rather than for sewing.

10

Blackfoot dress with Coolidge-Dawes thimbles . . . . .
Note yoke of real beads.

Likewise, other items brought in by traders found new
uses in the hands of the Indian women.

Ross reports that in 1812-14, trading was carried on
with Flatheads and Pend d'Oreilles along the Clarks Fork
of the Columbia (probably in western Montana).

Pressure from eastern people or acquiring the horse
might have prompted the Blackfoot, Piegan and Bloods to
move westward in the latter part of the 18th century.

The Bloods occupied a northern section, while the
Blackfoot moved south along the eastern slope of the rock-
ies and drove the Shoshone people out of what is now
Montana around 1800. In doing this they also challenged
the hunting rights of the mountain valley peoples such as
Flathead (Bitterroot-Salish), the Upper Pend d'Oreilles and
their northern neighbors, the Kootenai.

The Kootenai tried in vain to reach Hudson Bay traders
to obtain guns but the Blackfeet thwarted every attempt.

The Flatheads were not inclined to give up their traditional spring and fall buffalo hunting on Montana plains.

11

but their bows and arrows were useless against Blackfoot guns.

Not only did the Blackfeet deny the mountain valley people their hunting privileges, but they took special pleasure in raiding their home valleys. Because of their common enemy, these groups formed a loose alliance, which probably influenced a later decision to put them on the same reservation.

Wars are always carried on at the expense of the accumulative wealth of the peoples involved. The Blackfeet were quite affluent and could release men and material from family or tribal duties for raids on their neighbors, especially their western neighbors.

Needless to say, when Cox and his company arrived in western Montana, the traffic in guns and ammunition was brisk.

With guns the western people went 'over the Hill' to hunt. This time they shot back at the Blackfeet. This turn of events so enraged the Blackfeet that for many years they refused to allow American traders in their territory until the early 1840's when Fort Benton was established.

The conflict between the Western Tribes and the Blackfeet lasted possibly seventy-five years. Beginning around 1800, it was still going on by 1850. Jesuit Missionaries settled in the Bitterroot Valley in 1841, but sold out in 1850 because of the threat of the Blackfeet. Major Owens bought their mission and established a trading post. In 1855 Owens was instrumental in arranging for the Treaty of 1855 which established the Flathead Reservation. This area was the traditional home of the Upper Pend d'Oreilles and caused them no great anguish except the sharing of their dwindling resources. The Kootenai were located mainly in northwestern Montana and in Canada, west of Glacier Park. They did not move onto the Reservation until activities of outsiders forced them to do so in 1890. They settled for the most part in the northern portion around the community of Elmo.

Some of the Flatheads moved from the Bitterroot in 1872; others stubbornly refused to move for many years. Most of these people settled in the Jocko-Arlee area. These three groups today are commonly called Flathead.

The economics of these people--the Western Tribes and the Blackfeet--can explain many things to be found in their handcraft.

The Blackfeet were the power of the upper Missouri

12

River with horses, guns and buffalo. Their affluence allowed them to field numerous expeditions for wars and raids. Handcrafts flourished. Their choices of colors were bright with strong contrasts, as if reflecting their sunlit land. When the buffalo suddenly disappeared from the prairies of Montana and Canada, their economy went from affluence to desperate poverty in a couple of years.

The Western people were never as affluent, but they managed a comfortable living in spite of the raiding Blackfeet. They, much more than the Blackfeet, relied on plant products.

It is said that they used over twenty-six different plants for food and medicine. Their main meat diet was taken from small game animals such as deer. The mountain areas were never as plentiful with elk as were the eastern foothills.

The Western people were not as totally dependent on the buffalo as were the Blackfeet. Therefore, their economic decline was much more gradual. Western tribes suffered most from outsiders--miners and ranchers--who took many of their game animals and much of their natural plant foods. Reports indicate that outside traffic had drastically reduced the wild meat supply in the Bitterroot valley by 1860.

Perhaps this ever-diminishing supply of meat and leather caused the Flatheads to adopt cloth backing for much of their beadwork around 1880-1900.

The color choices of the mountain valley people seem to be somewhat somber, in comparison to Blackfeet.

Prehistorically many and various materials were fashioned for personal adornment such as stone, pebbles, bones, seashells, claws of birds and animals, horns, feathers and porcupine hair and quills. Every geographic area provided material that ingenuous people could utilize. New materials were quickly incorporated into their traditional handcraft.

For some reason applique beads were late in reaching Indian craftsmen.

John C. Ewers' paper, "Blackfeet Craft" will be used as reference and authority as it is assumed that his beadwork periods will be applicable to the Flathead area with slight exceptions.

Mr. Ewers uses three periods, which we quote: "The first period may be termed the pre-embroidery or bead necklace period, during which large beads were used to make

13

necklaces, bracelets, fringe decorations and hair ornaments"
.... 'The second period opened with the use of the embroidery bead among the Blackfeet. It may be termed the 'real bead' period." Of the third period Mr. Ewers says, "We may date the seed bead period from the year 1875..."

As previously stated, necklace beads were in use by 1800. It is possible the real bead period started about 1840. It is interesting to note that many older Blackfeet still use the term 'real" to denote things they consider of high quality or value.

There is an exception with the Flathead beading and use of the real bead. Either they considered the "real bead" a Blackfoot bead, an enemy bead, or else their low economy would not provide this luxury. At least there is not the evidence of extensive use of real beads by the Flatheads as there was by the Blackfeet.

During the real bead period the Blackfeet were enjoying their most prosperous time.

The seed bead period came near the end of the buffalo and the end of Blackfeet affluence. The Blackfeet seemed to prefer a medium sized seed bead to blend with their real bead designs while the Flatheads preferred a very small bead.

Changes in decorative designs accompanied each of these bead periods. The use of porcupine quills was widespread in prehistoric times. The master craftsmen had perfected traditional geometric designs for their respective groups. Real beads were used to enhance or enlarge quill work, later replacing much of the quill work. Certain uses of beads still reflects the earlier quill designs.

The master craftsman soon developed new geometric designs to better utilize the real bead. This process was repeated again when seed beads became available.

Not only were new and more complicated geometric designs developed, but also floral designs began to spread among various tribes. Approval of the floral designs by traders and other white people had great influence on its development. By 1900 floral design was predominant. If old quill work had special religious symbolism incorporated with the design, it must surely have been lost by the frequent transition of historic times.

Industrious women beaded then as they do today--in an effort to provide additional income for the family. They used the materials at hand to fashion their handcraft. The textiles the trader provided were incorporated into the hand-

14

craft in many ways. Thinking the white man's cloth was something extra fine, the craftsmen lined many things with gingham or calico. Needless to say, many a trader was at first shocked to see finely beaded articles, such as bags and gloves so adroitly lined with his cheap cloth.

The Indians discovered other possibilities for the cloth as well. During the 1860's, Fort Benton was doing a flourishing business with the Blackfeet. A large encampment had been set up with trading and the usual festivities in full swing. A Blackfoot mother allowed her teenage son to take a bolt of red cloth from the counter. This he promptly tied to his pony's tail and raced through camp and across the prairie. Startled ponies dumped their riders; shouts and screams followed.

It was not long before other ponies were flying across the prairie with a cloth banner flapping. Boys who could not find mother or cloth, chose to join the fun by riding across the banners to tear them loose. Some ponies refused to hit the cloth, shied suddenly, and sent the rider sailing. The fun ended with winded ponies, laughing people, a prairie littered with cloth and possibly some sober mothers who saw months of hard work laying wasted in the dust.

During the early trading days, the Indian dealt with the trader in the old Indian trading method. He took from his surplus and bartered for the things he did not have. He was shrewd in his dealings and usually satisfied that he had gained in the transaction. His gradual economic decline forced him to dip deeper into his material possessions, not to buy trinkets but things which had become necessities. He could no longer bargain in the old Indian style and was forced to accept the trader's terms. This eventually began a practice of pawning or hocking personal items and heirloom pieces of the family. These were to be redeemed if and when money or goods could be found for payment. Many women assumed the burden of redeeming articles by additional beading and tanning leather. They made many pieces during these more desperate times in a futile effort to fight back against economic depression, loss of social stature and degradation. Many priceless pieces came from this period. One can almost feel the stubborn pride and determination of the beading reflecting the plight of the people as they labored, scrimped and saved--some taking years to complete a piece of bead work.

The end was inevitable as valuable handcraft, piece by

15

piece, was lost to the Indian people. Present day collectors are finishing the job of picking up the last of the old pieces. Should the Indian people wish to reclaim some of their handcraft culture, they will pay dearly. For example, collectors have bid up to $4,000 for some of the old dresses.

Modern Indian handcraft has its finest moment at an Indian Pow Wow or War Dance for which occasions the dancers and some of the spectators are bedecked in a bewildering display of beadwork.

Modern dance outfits have merged to a certain uniformity for men and boys. Some items are of the old traditional design. For example, buckskin shirts are still worn by men of importance--mainly by Blackfeet and Canadian Bloods at special Indian ceremonies. The shirts are more tailored than the old style, with under-arm and side fringes of considerable length. A full eagle headdress is highly desirable to top off this outfit, but if one is not available a western "ten gallon" Stetson can be worn. Buckskin leggings with the traditional beaded side bands and full beaded moccasins and a colorful breechclout complete this "real" Indian outfit. No bells are worn with such an outfit.

The use of new materials and the old time method of exchanging ideas have played an important role in developing today's dance costume. There is the usual head piece, the roach. A yoke may be worn and a large feather bustle is common with or without two trailers of feathers, beads and cloth. Arm feathers are sometimes worn, arranged in a circle like a bustle, but with shorter feathers and plumes. An apron front and rear may replace the old breechclout, but occasionally a modified breechclout is worn. Knee bells, or rosettes of small feathers, and ankle bells with long-haired anklets are worn. Beaded moccasins are preferred with this outfit, but sneakers are also worn.

Ladies' costumes have remained more consistant with traditional patterns. Some tailoring has taken place, more cloth is being used and beaded high-top moccasins have replaced most of the old beaded leggings. A beaded headdress is very common. Buckskin dresses are still the most popular attire. These dresses are weighty by themselves, but when fully beaded and decorated, the weight is considerable.

Numerous items and methods can be used to complete a garment's decorations, as one is inclined, or as one can

16

afford.   As with all handcraft, no two outfits are ever
alike, except with regard to basic construction.

In the earlier days Indian garments, while showing
some tribal distinction, seemed to stem from a basic pattern and construction.   Uncluttered practicality seemed to
rule the Indian world and clothing was made of materials
available.   If small skins were available, the garment was
made of two skins joined with a simple shoulder-sleeve
seam.   If large skins were available, this seam was not
needed.   Sides were closed with or without fringes.   Men's
sleeves were always closed by sewing; women's were not.

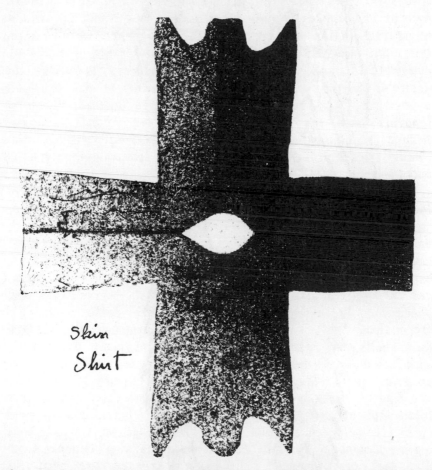

Skin
Shirt

The above cut-out of a skin shirt, along with following
ones of a 'britch clout' and a 'skin leggon' are the patterns referred to in the letter on page 2.   They were cut
from heavy brown wrapping paper.

Britch Clout
red blue or
green
flannel
one foot wide
4 feet long

Above cut-outs and sketch by C. M. Russell

A common basic pattern was used to make a woman's dress. In Southern climates it was usually a two piece garment, sleeveless, with a shoulder seam and a side seam. This dress had another cape-like piece, that fell over the arms to about elbow length (see illustration). In Northern regions, the dress and cape units became one. It was a two piece pattern using larger skins, so that the top line (shoulder-sleeve line) could be about three and a half feet long. The sides were cut and sewed in a straight line, starting about midway between the shoulder and the hip. This left a large opening under the arm.

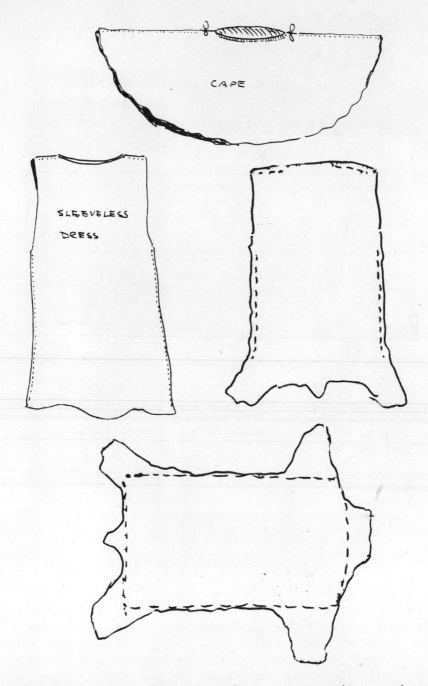

CAPE

SLEEVELESS DRESS

Illustrations above show sleeveless two-piece dress and cape and show how the dress was cut from two small skins. With very small skins, almost the entire skin was used, leaving the lower edge untrimmed. This would apply to garments for both men and women.

21

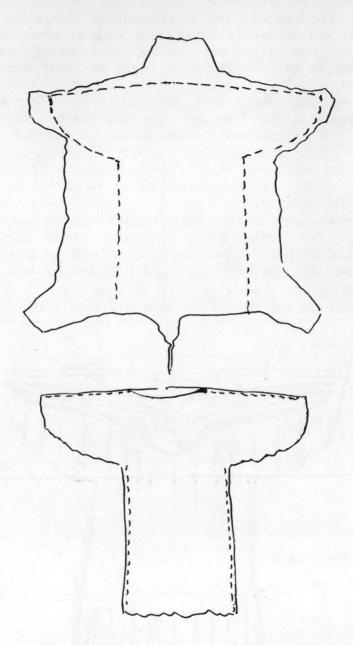

Medium sized skins would allow for trimming and for arm covering on women's dresses. Two pieces were joined along the shoulder-sleeve line and down the sides.

There were several practical reasons for this type of dress. The cape-like arm cover could be thrown back to bare the arm as needed during such work as removing the 'plumbing' from an animal carcass, or a nursing mother could merely shift the garment to serve an infant dinner at any time.

A belt was always worn with this dress. This bound the garment to the body and supported pouches for work tools. (A working woman made almost constant use of a cutting tool of stone or steel.) This traditional belt and pouch are still very much a must in modern celebration dresses. They may be of buckskin or cloth, but are now mainly decorative pieces.

Women's work dresses were simple, untrimmed and unfringed. But 'Sunday Best' were given careful attention. The shoulder-sleeve seam was covered with a decorative band and the cape-like sleeve was incorporated with the yoke design to produce a very pleasing effect. These areas received the bulk of the quill and bead work.

Shoulder-sleeve bands   Collar trim   Yoke design

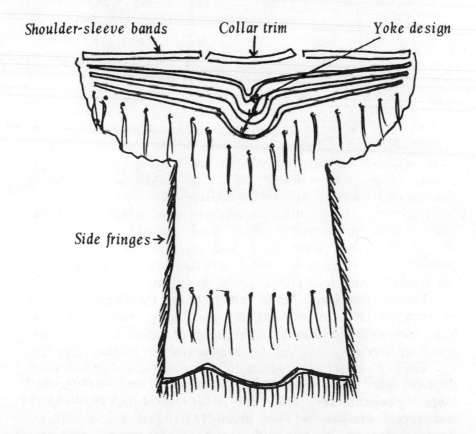

Side fringes →

The shoulder-sleeve seam of men's formal attire was covered with decorative bands, as well. These bands, sometimes in combination with other decorations, comprised the main decorations for men's shirts (see illustration). The social standing of a woman often hinged on how well she decorated and cared for her husband's formal attire.

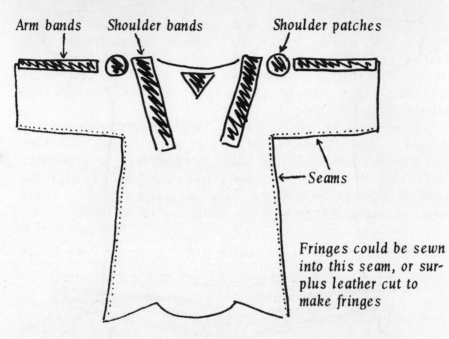

Arm bands   Shoulder bands   Shoulder patches

Seams

Fringes could be sewn into this seam, or surplus leather cut to make fringes

As has been indicated, not all Indian clothing was decorated; work clothing was not. The practical Indian mind did not find it sensible to waste time on such garments, if any were worn at all. (It should be remembered that prehistorically and historically, men and boys were 'half-naked'. Their various activities found clothing a hindrance except in winter.) When work was to be done, all the trinkets and finery were laid aside. If the day required no labor, or if a social function was to be had, all the trinkets and decorations could be worn.

Formal functions, Indian ceremonies, Pow-Wows and so on required full clothing and all the finery, particularly for head men and dignataries. The role of handcraft as a personal decoration could not be overlooked in Indian etiquette.

When a chief or headman of a group was called upon to represent the people before strangers, such as another Indian group, trader, army officer or the like, the dignity and social standing of the group rested on his shoulders. He must present himself with the best the group could pro-

24

vide.   If his personal gear was not adequate for some
reason, a borrowed substitute would be made.

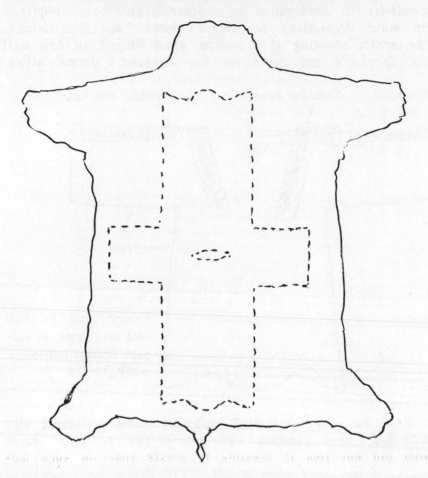

Large skins such as from elk, moose and young buffalo
would be needed to provide material for this type of shirt. These
would tan out about five feet by seven feet for the elk, or seven
feet by eight feet for the moose.

Much work was required to dress the leather to a uniform
thickness for clothing. A one piece shirt such as Russell shows
would speak well for the industry of the Blackfeet women.

The Western tribes preferred this weight material for tipi
covers, as the light weight deer skin was too sensitive to mois-
ture. It became soggy from evening condensation or rain.

Buffalo hides required the most work because of their size
and thickness. Large hides were split down the back and later
tanned and sewed together if used for robes and the like. Another
reason for splitting the hide was to be able to process half or
more of the carcass before rolling it over to get to the other side.

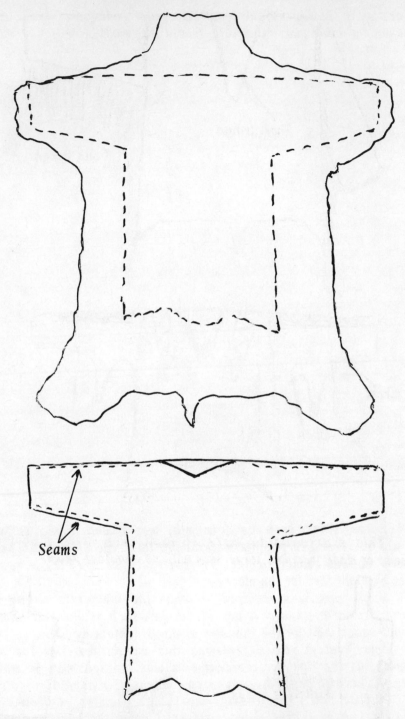

Seams

26   Men's two piece shirt, cut from medium size skins.   Fringes
were used under arms and on sides if desired and if material was
available.

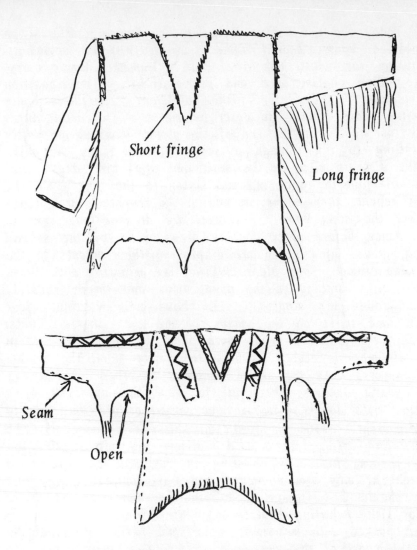

Short fringe

Long fringe

Seam

Open

This shirt could be made of small skins-with a shoulder seam-or made from one large skin with no shoulder seam.

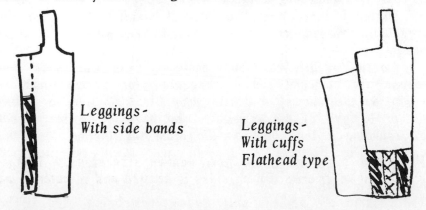

Leggings-
With side bands

Leggings-
With cuffs
Flathead type

Today the usual Pow Wow or War Dance starts at an appointed hour, 'Indian Time', which may be somwhat different from white man time. The Drummers arrive carrying folding chairs, drum and drum sticks. They position themselves in the center of the pavillion. Spectators begin to find seats around the outer perimeter. The head singer may tap lightly on the rim of the drum, humming or softly whistling to run through a song. When ready, he will strike a sharp blow on the drum and start his song. Others will join the drumming and listen to the tune. On the first repeat, they chime in and it is repeated three times before the song ends. Children are dressed and sent to the dance before older dancers dress. So by the second song, groups of children are displaying their talents to the growing crowd. Soon older children are mingling with them. Older girls dancing in the usual twos and threes sedately step around the singers. The boys with youthful vigor whirl and twist as they move around the singers counter-clockwise. Between songs more bells are heard jingling in the distance as others approach to slowly swell the number of dancers. As the crowd becomes absorbed in watching the young dancers, they fail to hear the approach of a mature male dancer. He may be young or old, but this is his moment. With the first beat after the introduction he bolts into action like a wild stallion, his bell beating out the rhythm, his body twisting in rhythmic contortions or upright he may prance around and cast haughty looks over his shoulders. Others soon join the dance to add more color, with whirling bodies and flying feet. The area is soon packed with movement, color and bells--all pulsating to the boom of the war drum. During such a melee one might expect some violent collisions to occur but seldom if ever is there body contact.

During a large Pow Wow several singing groups may be present, each singing a set of songs and waiting for their turn.

Dozens of different songs may be sung and those that please the dancers can be repeated for several dances, either on the cue of a dancer who blows a flute or whistle or by one of the drummers who signals another repeat by sounding a loud beat on the drum the instant the song ends. The Flathead once used over twenty-two different types of songs in their pattern of living. Most of these have gone the way of much of the old Indian culture. Today there are perhaps only three types being used. The

28

War Dance songs, Owl Dance songs and a few still use the 'Stick Game' songs. The Owl Dance (round or Grass Dance) seems to be a more recent historical development though the tempo of the drum beat may be from older dances.

This tempo with its soft then heavy beat signals the dancers to arrange themselves in a large circle facing the singers. They join hands as the singing starts. They lead to the left (clockwise), on the soft beat, with a short step and bring up to the right on the heavy beat. There is a slight pause in the beat which is used to initiate the next step. Knees are slightly flexed with each step so the entire circle dips in unison. Many on-lookers join in this dance; the line can become very long. The line is sometimes reversed by a lead dancer who will turn facing outward still moving to his left.

In another version of this dance beat, couples join hands and dance forward instead if sideways.

Indian social functions such as celebrations and ceremonies date back into antiquity. Though many forms and types have been lost, the general custom prevails in spite of desperate times and interference by both government and church. On such occasions the display of personal decorations has been of prime importance throughout the centuries. During the early reservation days when people could still remember their former glory and good life, their handcraft was a visual reminder of their loss. Since then handcraft, mainly beadwork, has become an identity symbol.

Handcraft, the world over, is probably the least offensive of expressions between men. Indian handcraft is readily acceptable to the dominant white society, and in some ways is perhaps the most acceptable contribution of Indian culture.

Indian Pow Wows of today, though they represent an ancient Indian custom, have become an expression of identity for Indian people. The Pow Wow without Indian handcraft would be like playing symphonic music for the deaf.

Demands of Indian people and non-Indian people have kept the craft alive, but present day economics present a somewhat doubtful future.

Beading Techniques

The methods and means of using beads are many and varied. Beading done on background material such as buckskin or cloth will vary as to method, depending on the use of the finished article. Beading done without background support must lock the beads in place by thread alone.

The tying of beads to a background material can vary from tying each bead, every other bead, every three beads or they can be strung in loops of ten or more before tying. See illustrations.

Edging beads, when used, should be tied with a double thread as these beads receive considerable wear.

A very common method is the 'Lazy Stitch'. This is a fast way to bead and where the article is not subjected to intensive use it is quite satisfactory. Depending on the wishes of the beader, the design in mind, the size of the beads, any number of beads from four to twelve can be strung on each loop. Because of the variations in beads the long loops should be checked for length before tying the loop. When this is done, a new group of beads are threaded and laid along side the first row, the needle going through the backing as close to the first row as possible and back up through the backing to the bead side.

The thread should be snug but not too tight as it can bow the backing and distort the design to follow. This method will be followed to the end of the bar of the design. Changes in bead color will be made as the bars are laid up the work. By using the following patterns it will be easy to pick up the bead changes as the design develops. Each rectangle of the graph represents a bead space. If the proper bead size is used the finished design should have the same proportions as the drawing.

'Lazy Stitch'

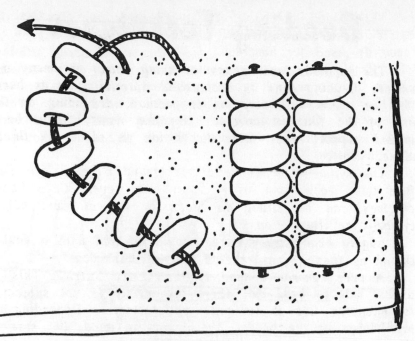

Another view of 'Lazy Stitch'

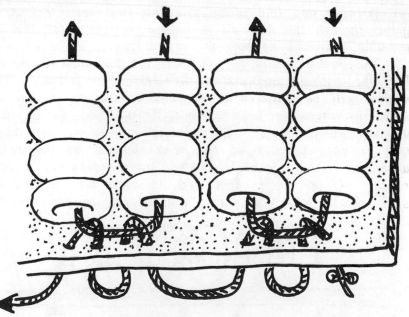

Modified 'Lazy Stitch'

The 'Overlaid Stitch' is used where the use of the article requires more tightly held beads. This stitch is commonly used for handbags and other much used articles. Most floral work requires regular tying down of the beads. Certain places require tying each bead, others are tied every two or three beads. This method needs two needles and thread. One is used to carry the beads, the other is used to bring loops over the carrying thread as shown in the illustration.

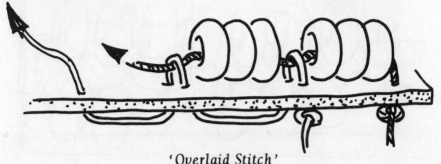

'Overlaid Stitch'

Another stitch could be called the 'Return Stitch', as the thread is brought back one, two or three beads, passing through the beads a second time before picking up the next beads. This may be at random selection if one wishes. It has some advantage over the Overlaid Stitch as only one needle is used, and beads can be as firmly held.

All of these stitches can be used on the same piece if a person so desires, or even other variations might be employed. For instance, the Lazy Stitch can be modified and a second thread used to tie the loops of beads.

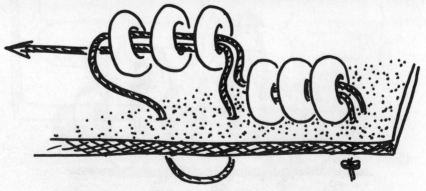

'Return Stitch'

Edging beading can be done in several ways. The most common seems to be to pass from the edge through two beads, back through the edge, back through the last bead, thread two beads, leave one free and back through the lower bead, the edge and back through the last bead, thread two beads and repeat until the edge is finished. See illustrations.

This can be varied by the number of beads used along the edge and in the outer loop.

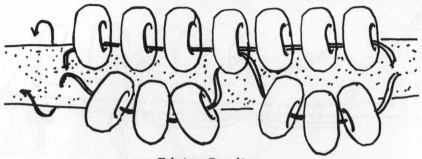

Edging Beading

Beads without backing material can be strung by several methods. One method with an oblique effect can produce some interesting geometric designs. This can be started by tying a row of beads loosely to an edge. Each bead must be tied. At the end of the run the needle is passed back through the first bead, through a loose bead, through the second bead, through a loose bead, and so on to the end. If the return run must pass through the last bead a loose bead is strung to hold the thread. This process is repeated and different colors added as the band grows. See illustration.

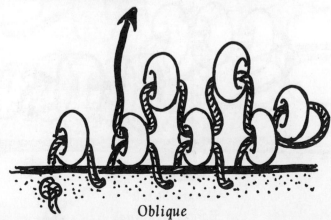

Oblique

33

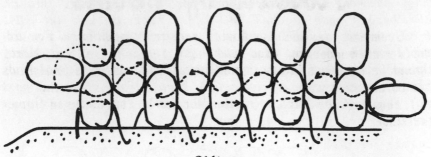

Oblique

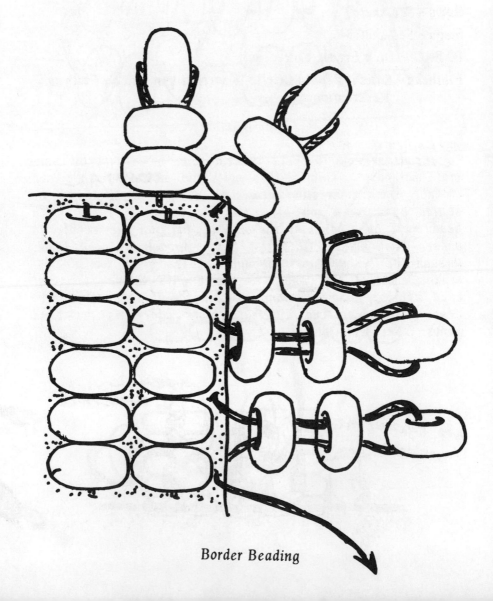

Border Beading

Glossary of Terms

Geometric designs sometimes require 'crowding'. For example - even numbered bead rows - 2 - 4 - 6 - 8 - 10, etc., darts cannot be centered without 'crowding'. Odd numbered bead rows can be centered without 'crowding'. Floral designs, for the most part, require 'crowding', to tighten the work, especially in flower centers.

Loops - See sketch

Bars - See sketch

Rows - See sketch

Steps - See sketch

D. E. C. - Dick Ereaux Collection

Flathead - Salish, Pend d'Orielle, Kootenai enrolled on Flathead
        Reservation.

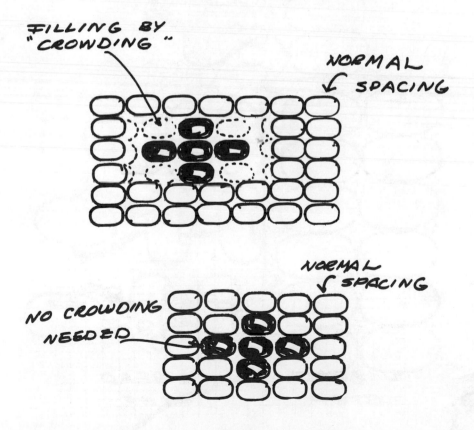

FILLING BY "CROWDING"

NORMAL SPACING

NO CROWDING NEEDED

NORMAL SPACING

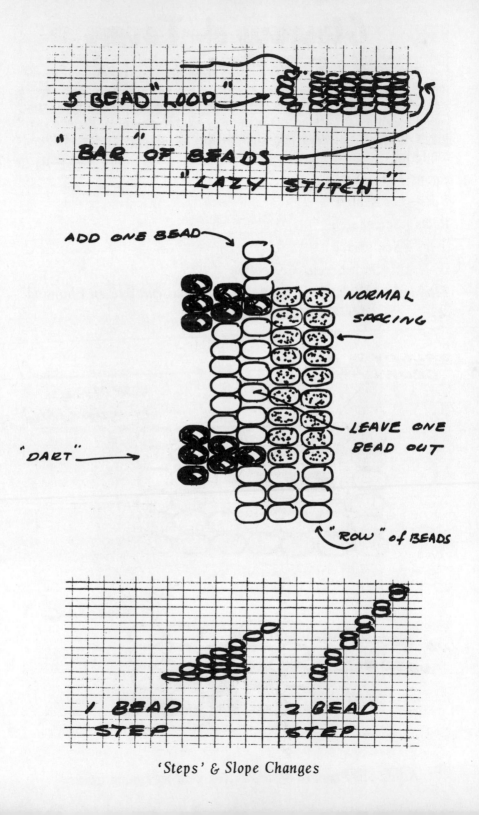

5 BEAD "LOOP"

"BAR" OF BEADS

"LAZY STITCH"

ADD ONE BEAD

NORMAL SPACING

"DART"

LEAVE ONE BEAD OUT

"ROW" of BEADS

1 BEAD STEP

2 BEAD STEP

'Steps' & Slope Changes

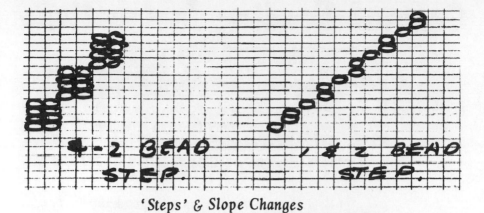

'Steps' & Slope Changes

A fine old example of decorating with porcupine quills

General Beading Instructions

1. MATERIAL LAYOUT

Many beaders cover a table or stand with a cloth and place beads and needles on this. The cloth holds beads and needles from rolling off and getting lost on the floor.

Shallow trays should be provided to hold the beads. Strung beads can be used directly from the string.

2. LIGHTING

Good lighting is very important.

3. COMFORT

Beading is tiring, so the chair and materials should be such as to reduce awkward or uncomfortable conditions.

If you do not have a pattern in mind, let us start with----

INSTRUCTIONS FOR SIMPLE
GEOMETRIC DESIGN BEADING

HEAD BAND

Prepare a strip of backing such as heavy cloth, suede or buckskin leather, about twenty-four inches long and one and one-half inches wide.

Thread beading needle with a thread about twenty-four inches long. It is better to use a short thread.

See Figure 1. Start from either left or right as you prefer, bring the thread up from the back side of the backing at Point A. Draw it up tight against the knot and tug it several times to see that it will not pull through.

Select a background color of white or pale blue beads. String eleven beads then push them to Point A. Lay the string of beads from Point A to Point B, be sure the beads are all touching.

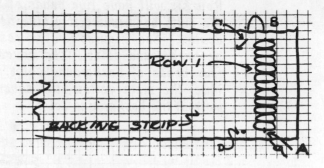

Figure 1

Sew into backing at Point B and return at Point C, string eleven beads and sew into backing at Point D. See Figure 2. Pull the thread up snug so that both rows of beads are touching and the beads in each row are touching. The looseness in the center of the rows will be taken care of later.

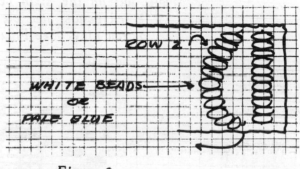

Figure 2

Continue this operation until five rows are done. See Figure 3.

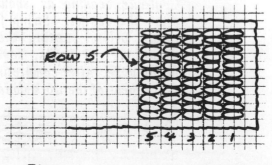

Figure 3

39

Row six will have five beads of background color, the sixth bead (make it a blue bead) will start the design. See Figure 4. The rest of the row will be background color. The seventh row will have four beads of background color, the fifth will be blue, the sixth yellow, the seventh blue and four more of the background color.

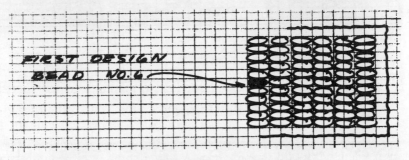

Figure 4

Continue these 'steps' to row nine. The red center bead will fall on the sixth bead. Row ten will have three red beads, row eleven will have one, the same as row nine. See Figure 5.

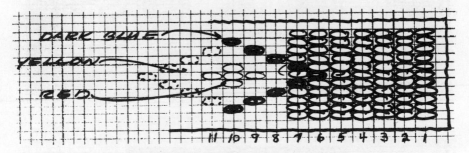

Figure 5

Continue beading as shown in Figure 6 to complete the design. String four rows of background beads before starting the cross design. This should be red beads, seven beads high and five beads wide. After completing the cross the beading is a repeat of the work done.

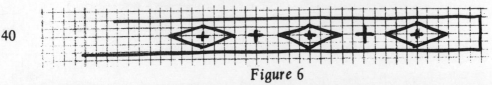

40

Figure 6

DESIGNS SUITED FOR BANDS - AND SMALL HAND BAGS

These designs can easily be enlarged by increasing the bead count per row. Odd number count, 7, 9, 11, etc. will provide better angles and points. See Figure 7.

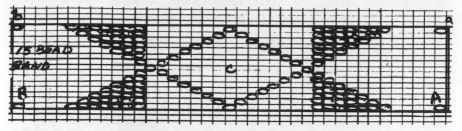

Figure 7

Figure 8

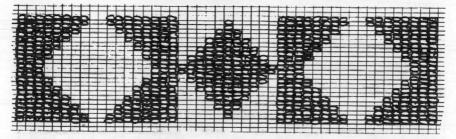

Figure 9   24 Bead Band

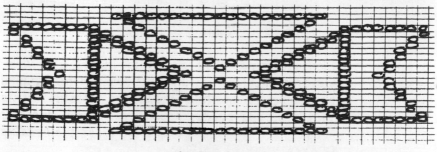

19 Bead Band

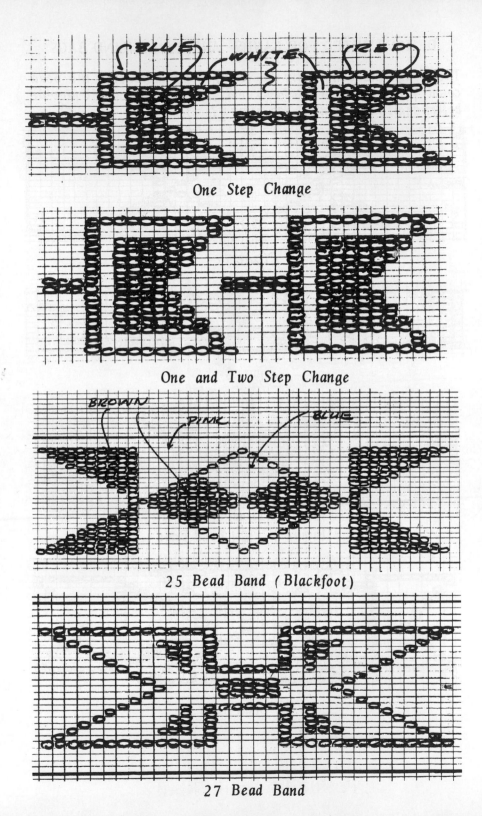

One Step Change

One and Two Step Change

25 Bead Band (Blackfoot)

42

27 Bead Band

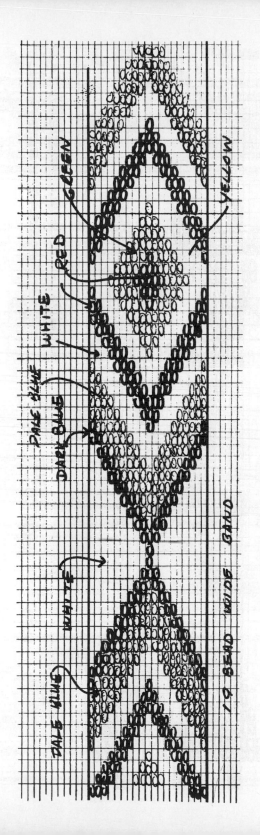

43

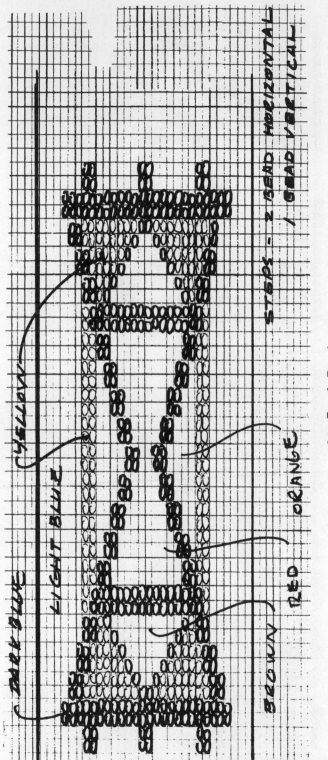

YELLOW

LIGHT BLUE

DARK BLUE

RED   ORANGE

BROWN

STEPS — 2 BEAD HORIZONTAL
/ BEAD VERTICAL

30 Bead Band

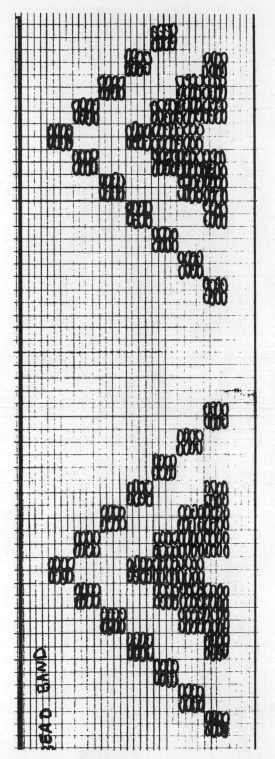

36 Bead Band

45

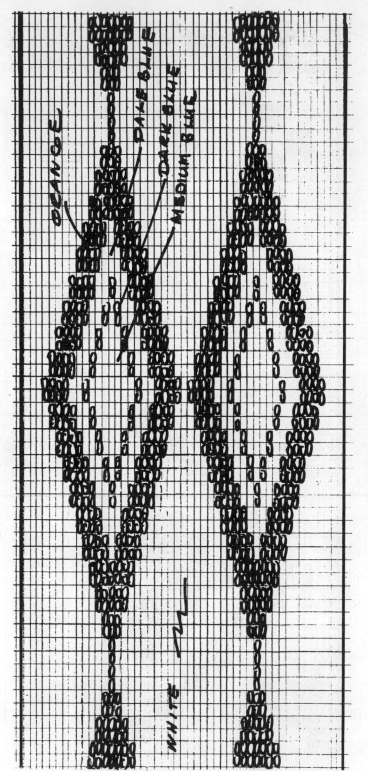

49 Bead Shoulder Band

46

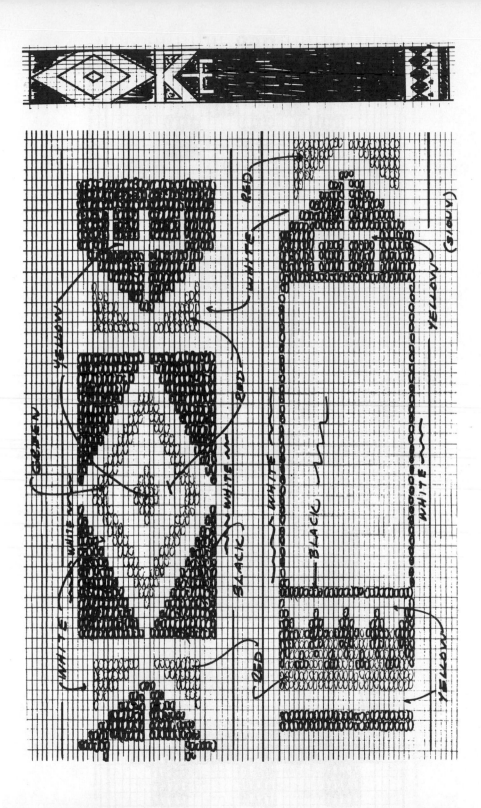

47

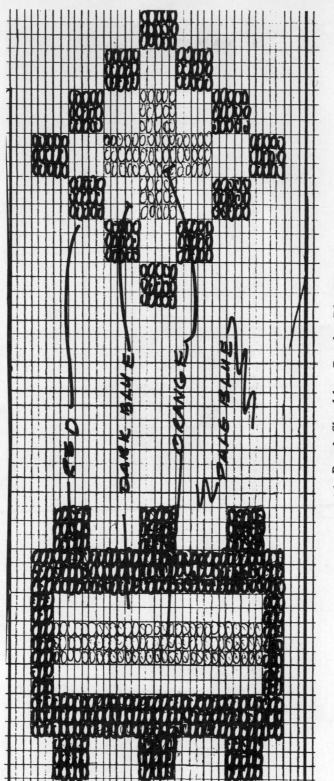

41 Bead Shoulder Band (Blackfoot)

48

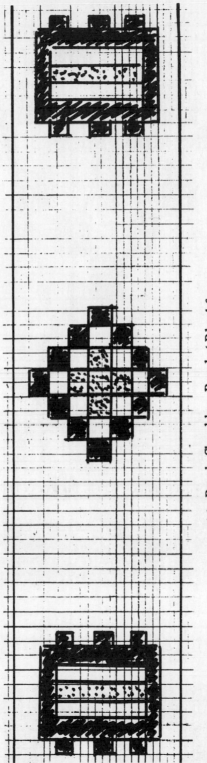

41 Bead Shoulder Band (Blackfoot)

49

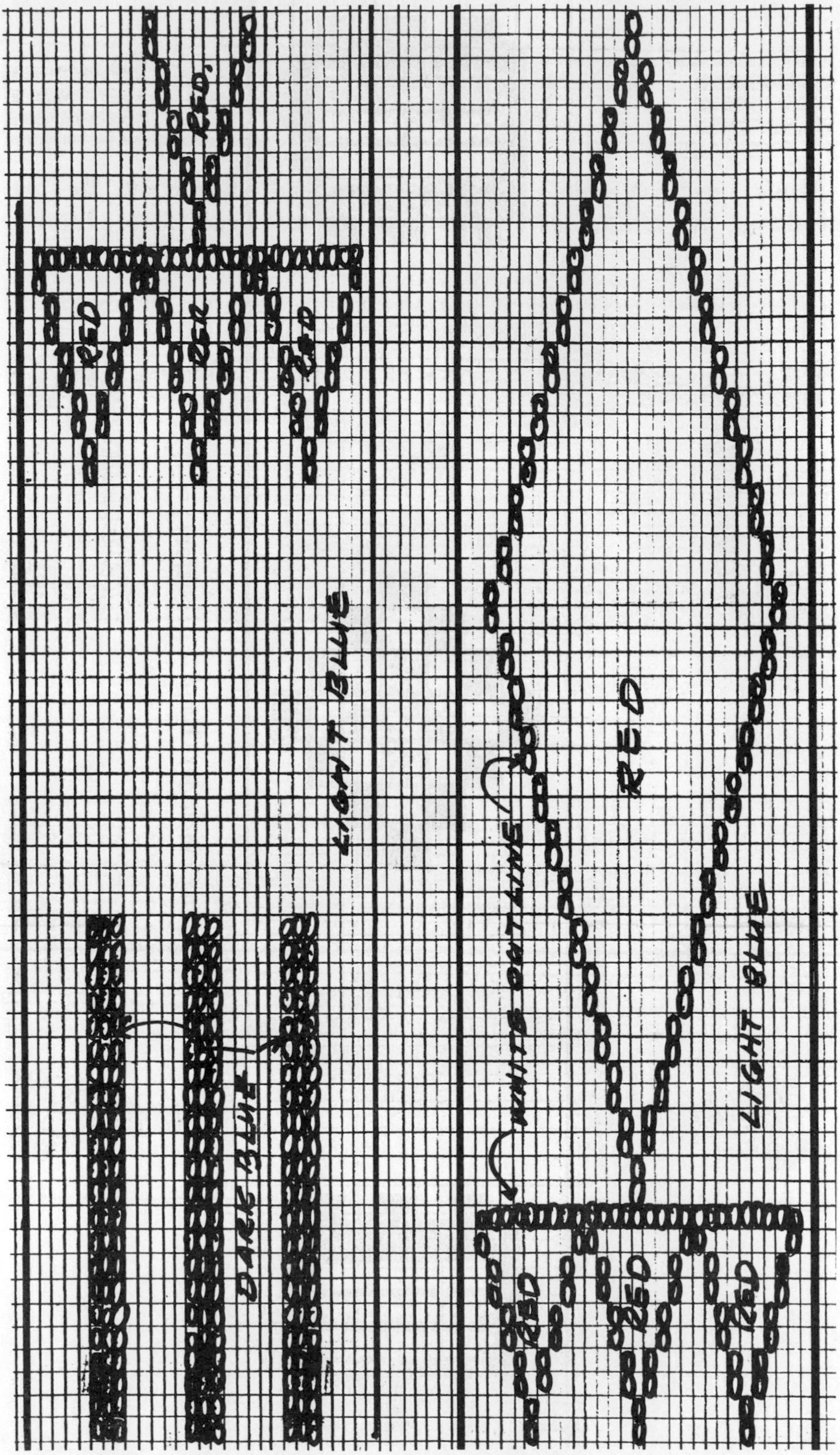
RED
RED
RED
RED
LIGHT BLUE
DARK BLUE
WHITE OUTLINE
RED
LIGHT BLUE
RED
RED
RED

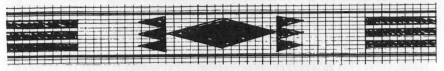

Above and at left: Shoulder band of Blackfoot design.
Enlarge by adding more rows. Keep two-bead step, lateral.

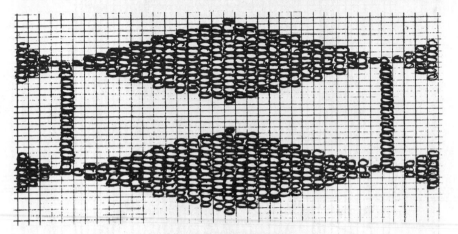

39 Bead Band

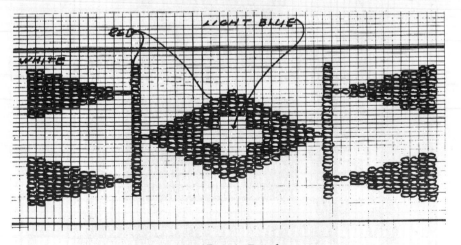

39 Bead Band

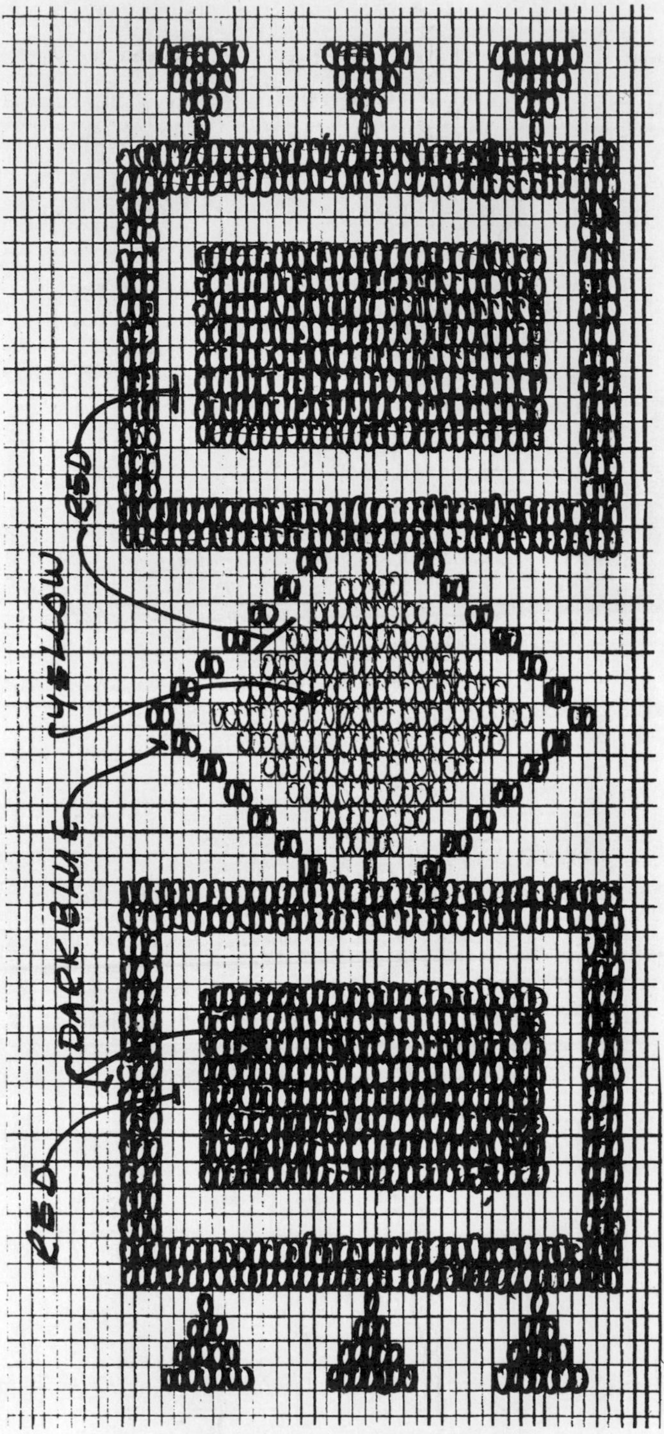
RED
YELLOW
DARK BLUE
RED

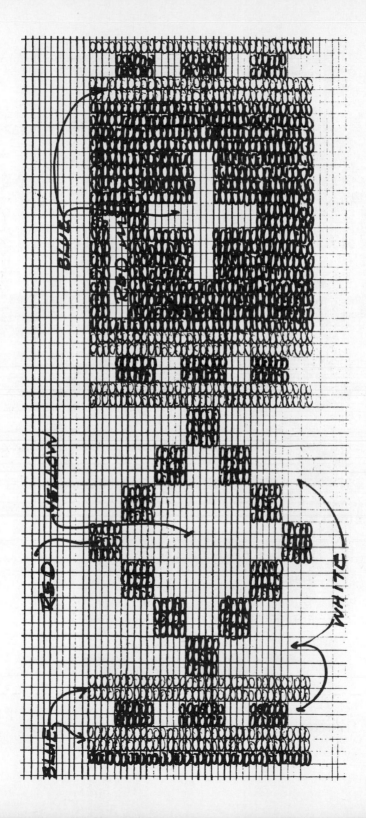

53

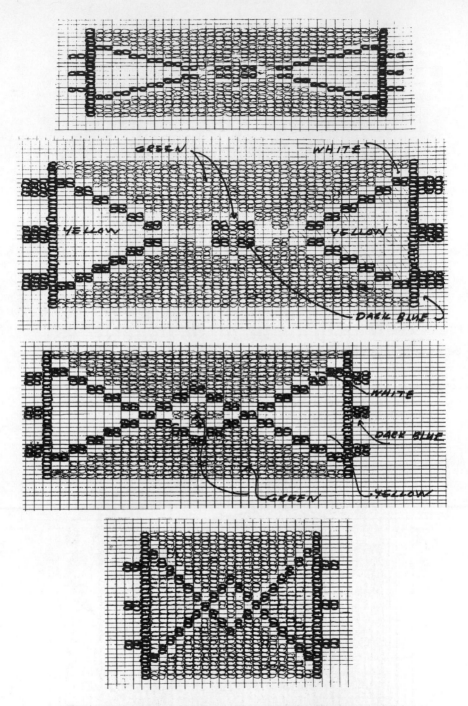

Showing some possible variations of a basic design.

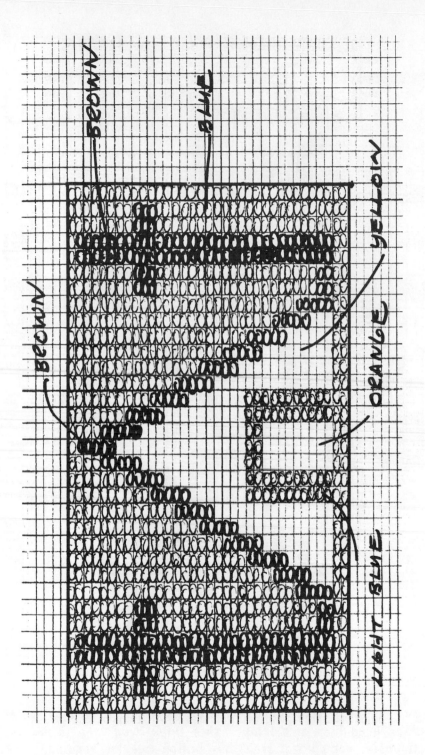

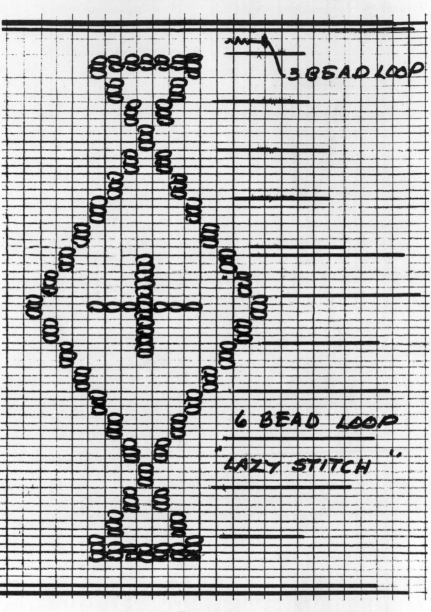

Figure A

Figure A can be made with a 'Lazy Stitch' six bead loop, with a three bead loop at the top. This three bead loop is not objectionable, nor does it break any Indian rule for beading. The three bead loop could be used in the center, also.

Figure B

Figure B shows the same design done with bead rows running
at right angles to those of Figure A. The proportions can be
changed by the changing of the lateral or vertical steps. The
center cross could be altered by using a one bead run instead of
two. A one bead run would require 'crowding' of beads inside
the diamond to center the cross. Note also the piece could
have a six bead loop with the five bead loops. It is hoped that
this will show the freedom possible with beading.

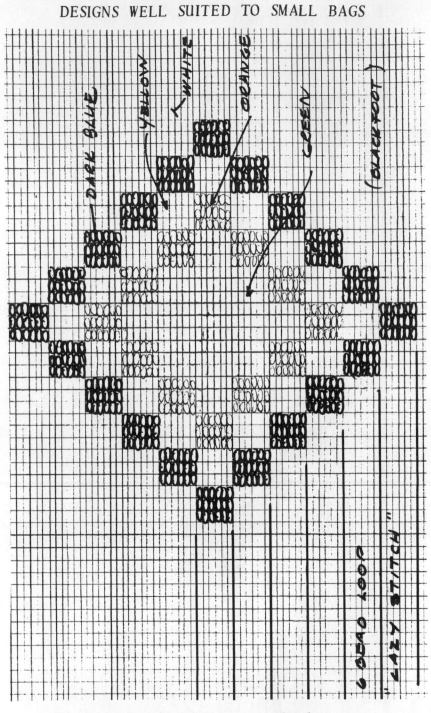

Design used on bags, dresses or other large areas

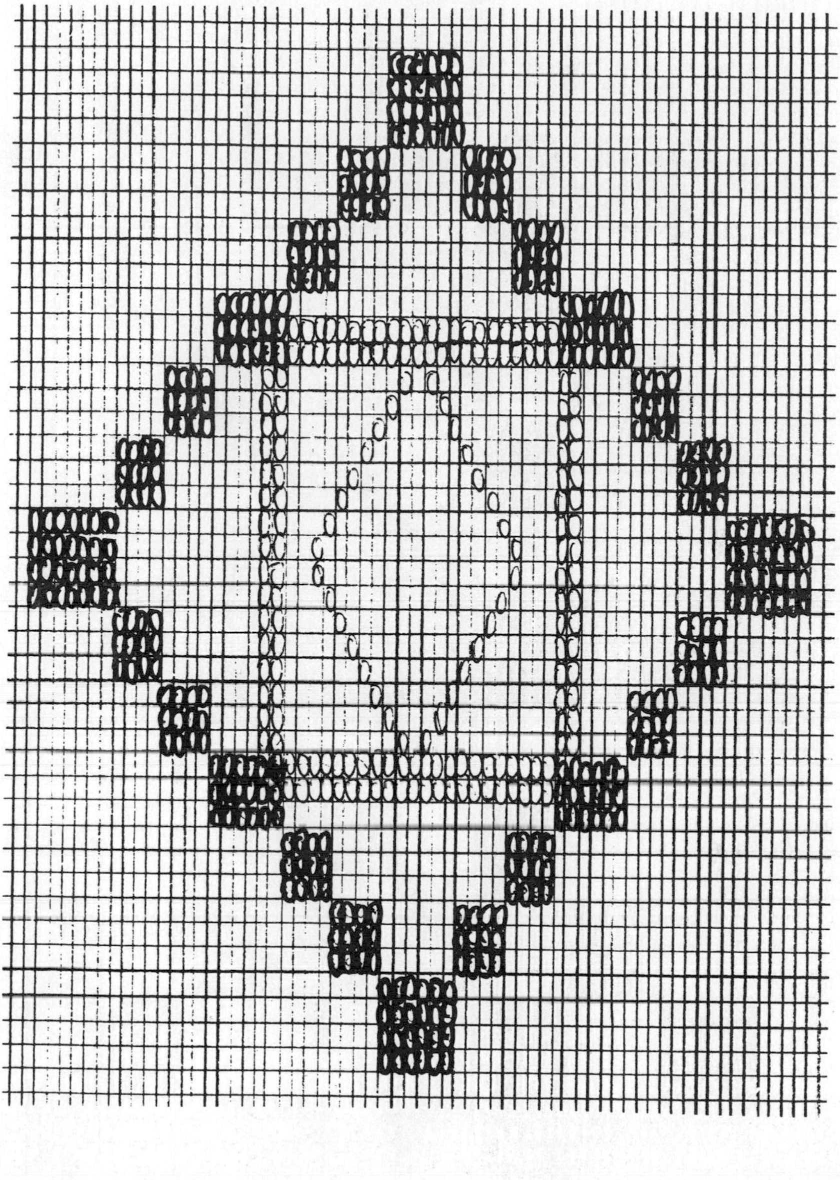

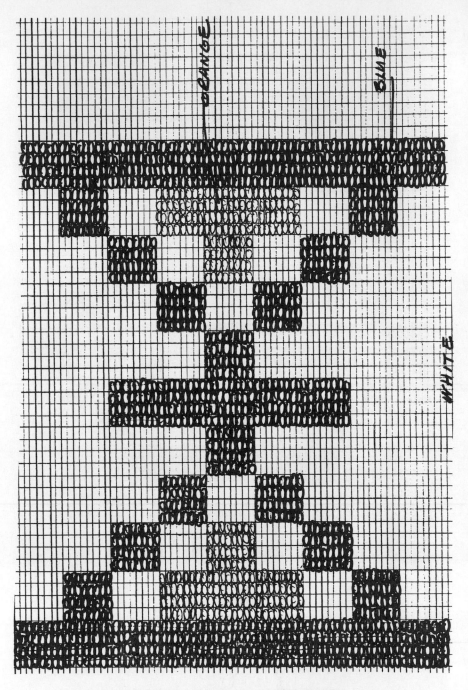

'Lazy Stitch' Bag Design

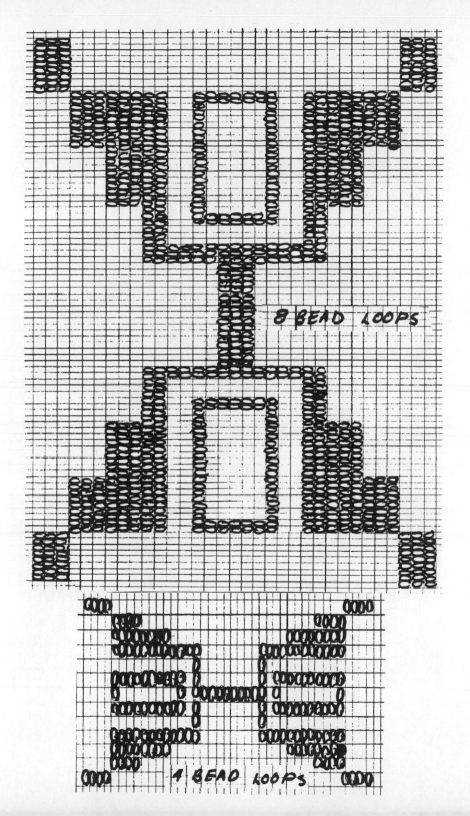

8 BEAD LOOPS

4 BEAD LOOPS

61

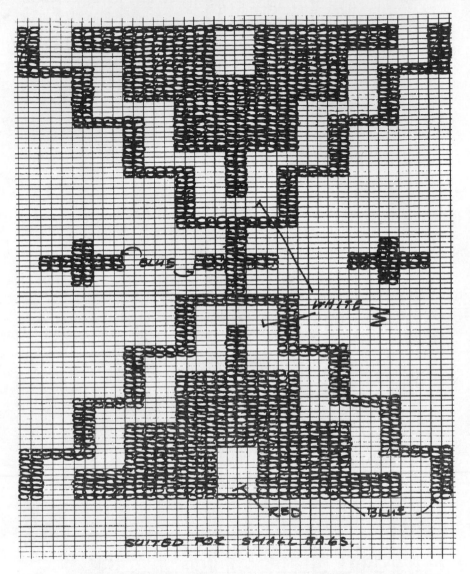

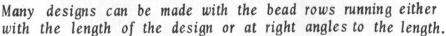

Many designs can be made with the bead rows running either with the length of the design or at right angles to the length.

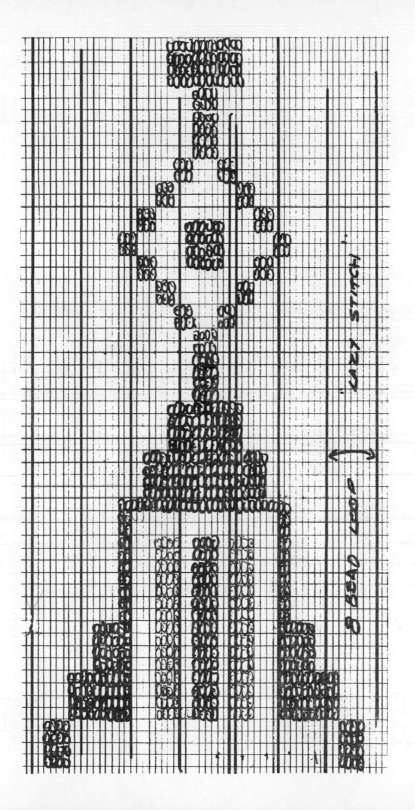

"LAZY STITCH".

8 BEAD LOOP

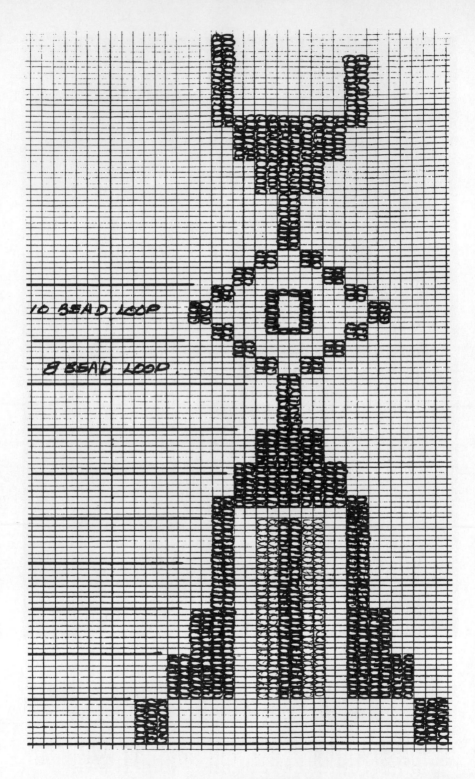

10 BEAD LOOP

8 BEAD LOOP.

Small bag made by Mary Finley (Flathead) in 1970. Mary should be considered to be a Master Craftsman. She is one of the oldest active beaders and still does excellent beading. Her work shows great sensitivity of color and beading skills. When color variations in beads are available she will balance color scheme with the color of the background material.

BEGINNING FLORAL BEADING

Select a floral pattern or use the one shown on this page. Transfer the pattern onto a piece of brown wrapping paper and pin this to a backing material. Arrange beads in flat trays or or dishes as before and use a short length of thread, about sixteen inches at the most. Bring the thread up to Point A, through backing and tracing of pattern. As there are three methods that can be used, we will explain each.

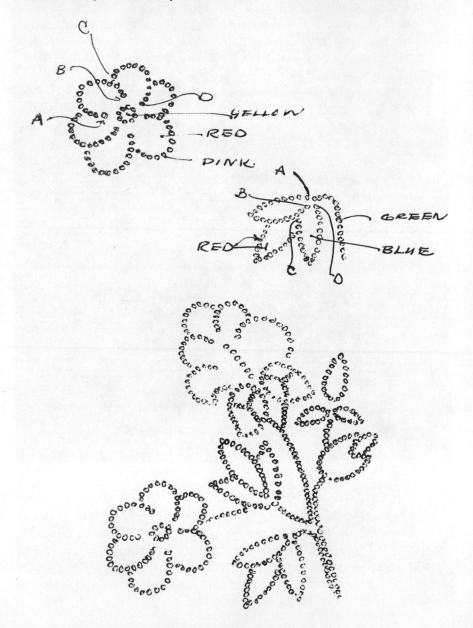

66

One way would be to string enough beads on the thread to cover the pattern line from A to B. The thread can be tied at Point B, on the back side of the backing. A second thread is now used coming up between beads one and two, looping over the 'carrying thread' and back through the backing and up again between beads two and three and so on, making certain that the beads are as close to each other as possible and that the second thread is kept snug. Continue this tying to Point B. Do the same for the loop between C and D, and for each petal. The same method can be used for the center of the flower.

Another method could be the usual overlaid stitch. Start at Point A, string several beads and push them to Point A. Bring a second thread up between the first and second beads as above and tie each bead as before.

The last method would be the 'return stitch'. Start as before at Point A. String two beads, bring them to Point A and run the thread through the backing as close as possible to the second bead, bring the thread back between the first and second bead, through the second bead the second time. String two beads and sew through the backing, back between the third and fourth beads, out through the fourth bead and so on. Pull the tying string snug after each return loop is made.

All floral designs can be made by these three methods. Feel free to select any one of them. The interior of the designs can be beaded in most any direction. See photos.

Photo at the bottom of the preceding page shows the detail of the large central flower of the bag on the front cover. This is a complicated flower pattern with an equilateral triangle as a base figure. To bead this the outline should be sewn as shown in the sketch, tying each bead firmly. The petal areas and center areas are filled with color changes as shown in the photo and the sketch below. One can see the individual treatment given each area. Background beads are sewn on last in straight rows. Note several areas where beads are crowded and even placed at various angles to fill a spot.

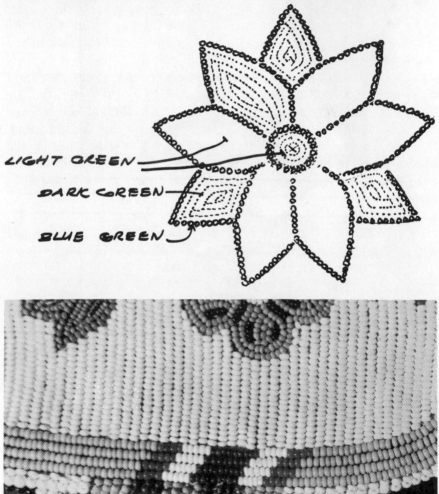

LIGHT GREEN

DARK GREEN

BLUE GREEN

Another detail of front cover photo. Note the change in direction of bead rows along the border in the four row border and the edging of six bead loops which was put on last, joining the front and back sections to produce a solid beaded exterior.

Detail of front cover photo. showing the design of the wrist strap. This is very good beading. Probably Flathead.

Close examination will reveal many areas of crowding and other interesting uses of beads. For example, the upper six-petaled flower shows individual arrangement of beads in each of the petals. The total effect is very pleasing.

Handcraft such as this shows a somewhat typical side of Indian life, where individuality prevails uninhibited by rules and regulations. Note also the carefully sewn cloth liner.

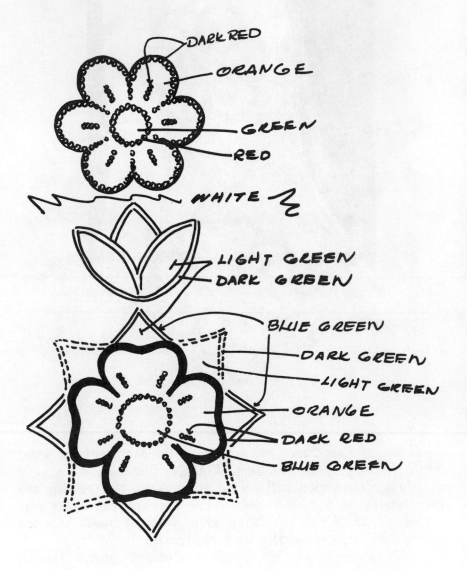

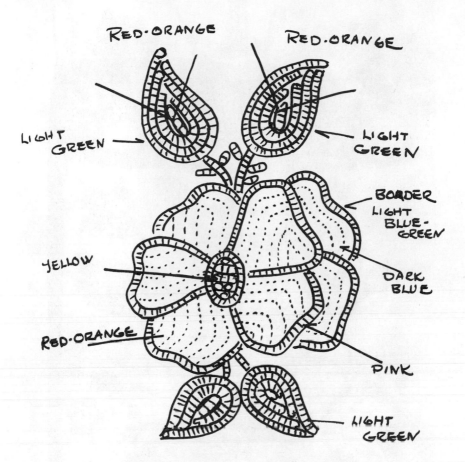

RED-ORANGE

RED-ORANGE

LIGHT GREEN

LIGHT GREEN

BORDER
LIGHT
BLUE-
GREEN

YELLOW

DARK
BLUE

RED-ORANGE

PINK

LIGHT
GREEN

Diagram of photo on Page 6 5.

A view of the pouch in the apron of a full beaded martingale worn around a horses neck during a festive occasion.

It is said that this type of article was once worn by medicine men as a bandolier, thus the pouch. Many of the old martingales have this traditional pouch.

This view shows many designs that could be copied by experienced beaders. Flathead D.E.C.

View of beaded strap which supported the apron-pouch.

Detail view of the excellent beadwork of the strap.

Photo of gauntlet cuff of Curly Ereauxs' gloves. (D.E.C.) These were made by Mary Pipe Woman (Gros Ventre) a master craftsman. These were probably made around 1900. The usual individual treatment shows in filling areas. NOTE - The beadwork is cleverly attached to 'store bought' gloves.

75

Another detail of gloves, showing in particular the border beading and the edging beads.

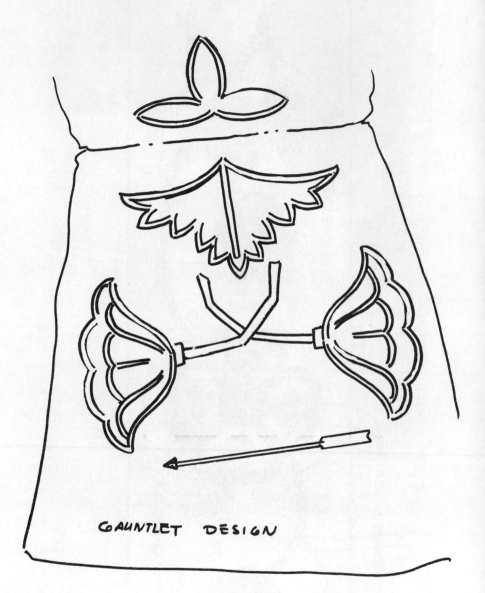

GAUNTLET DESIGN

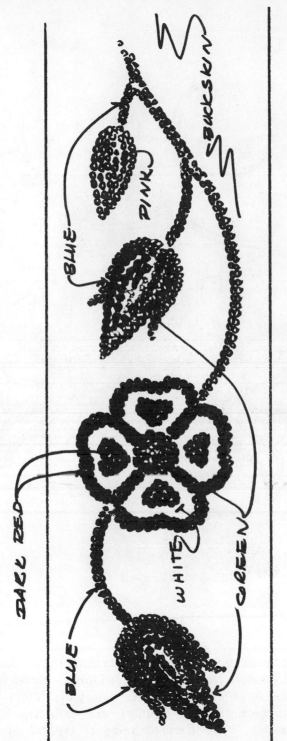

Band Design

One of the pieces given my father by Sally Anderson. Sally lived on the old DHS ranch Northeast of Lewistown, Montana, which was established by Granville Stuart. Sallys' father, Reese Anderson, was ranch foreman. Stuart and Anderson both took Snake Indian wives. The floral beading is typical of the late 1800s. The stitch is overlaid, every bead tied.

80

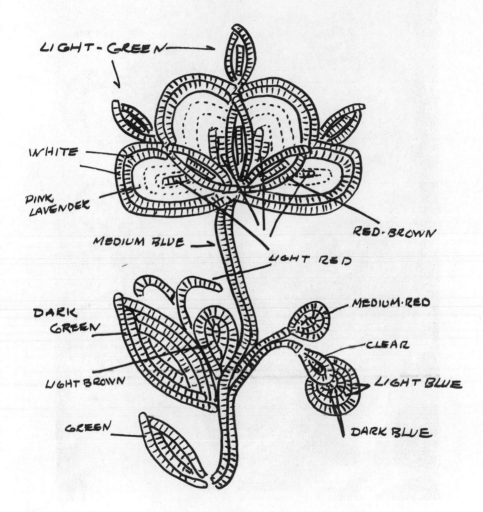

LIGHT-GREEN

WHITE

PINK
LAVENDER

MEDIUM BLUE

LIGHT RED

RED-BROWN

DARK
GREEN

MEDIUM-RED

CLEAR

LIGHT BROWN

LIGHT BLUE

GREEN

DARK BLUE

81

Reverse side of bag on page 80.

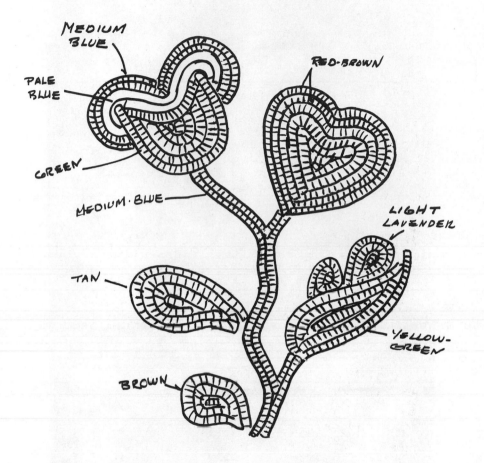

MEDIUM BLUE

PALE BLUE

GREEN

MEDIUM·BLUE

TAN

BROWN

RED-BROWN

LIGHT LAVENDER

YELLOW-GREEN

83

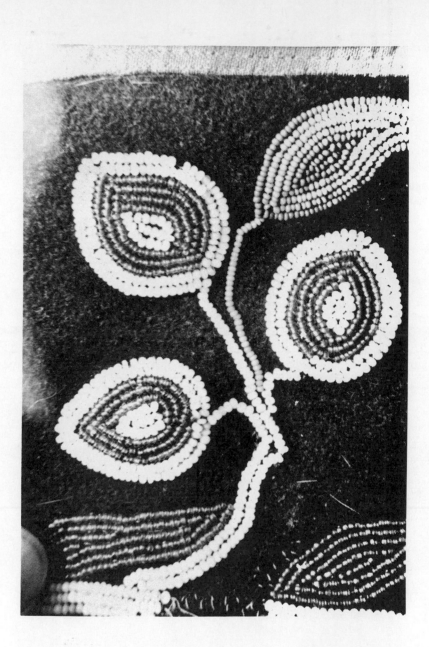

84   *Detail of Flathead floral beading on black wool. Note variations in bead size. Also note threads at lower right showing overlaid stitch was used. D.E.C.*

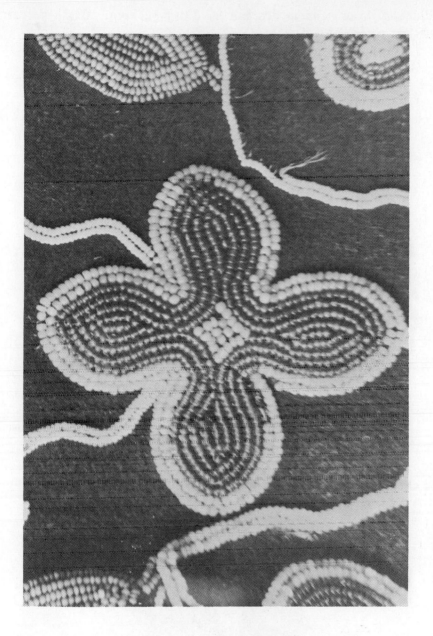

Another detail of same article.

85

Flathead floral beading designs for cloth backing. Black velvet
was the preferred material.

Band design from Jim Spencer collection.

89

Floral designs - done on cloth backing, suitable for large areas, such as the back of shirts, jackets, etc.

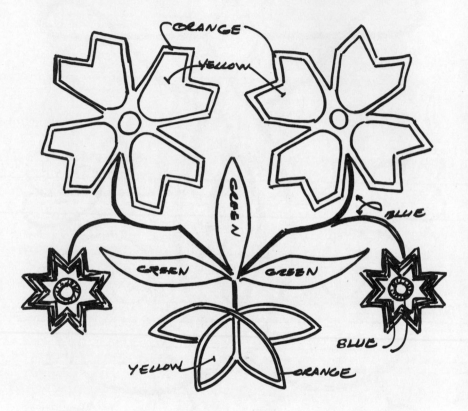

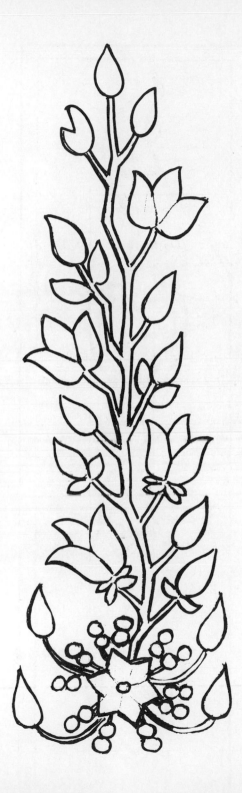

93

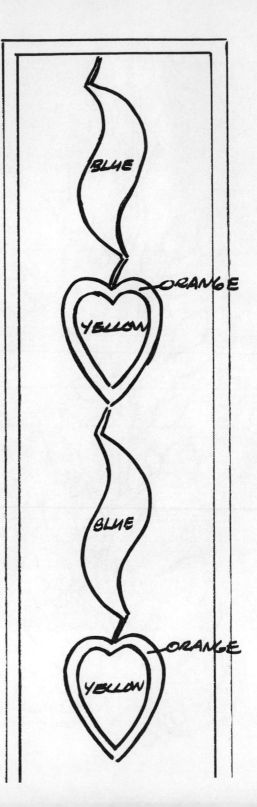

A *view of a necklace* Rosette *or* Medallion *recently beaded by*
Mary Finley. *Though a frail old woman she still does excellent*
beading. Note *the typical edging beading and the beaded cord.*

Flathead - Possibly the work of Mary Smallsalmon. Excellent example of triple rosette showing the interlocking edging beads. Also note the extension of edging beads to form the pendants. Color photo at right is same article.

Design from a beaded patch sewn on a Nez Perce corn husk bag. Note the variety of beads used and the freedom of design and the 'crowding' in various places. The resulting piece is not unpleasing.

A view of a Nez Perce medicine bag showing the intricate weaving of the bag and designs incorporated into it. This weaving is considered one of the lost arts of the Indian world. Lewis and Clark journals mention the Nez Perce skills in weaving.

There was considerable inter-tribal relationship between the Nez Perce and the Flathead. Nez Perce often joined Flathead friends on buffalo hunts, or spent years with one group or the other. Many of todays Flatheads have Nez Perce ancestry. D.E.C.

99

An interesting design. (Possibly Flathead) Note variations in bead sizes, the 'crowding' and edging loops. D.E.C.

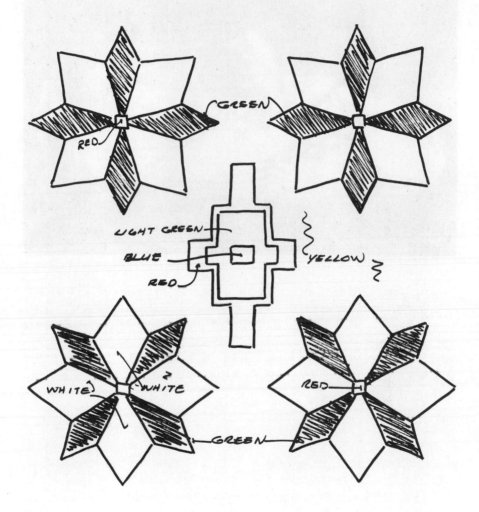

Moccasins

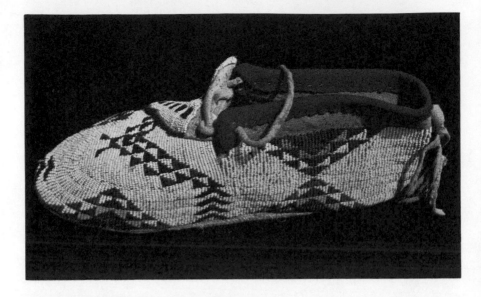

Moccasins were decorated in all sorts of manners. Various moccasin types offered a variety of areas for decoration. The seam of the Center Seam was covered, the insert of the Puckered Toe was decorated, the complete surface of the upper part of the Hard Sole and the Side Seam could be decorated. Special Hard Sole moccasins were completely covered with beading, soles as well as the upper part.

Quills were used hundreds of years before beads, and designs well developed that were suited to quill decoration. Many of these were easily transfered to bead work, or the quill work was bordered or interlaid with beads. Many of the traditional bars and rosettes were carried over into beadwork.

The most elaborate moccasin beading can be seen today at an Indian celebration.

The full beaded moccasins shown in the colored photo were made by Mary Pipewoman for Curly Ereaux around the turn of the century. D.E.C. The beading is the usual type used on Hard Soled moccasins.

Usually the full beaded moccasins were used only for special occasions and could last a lifetime. The less the decoration the more a moccasin was worn unless under dire conditions it was a necessity to wear something.

Above photo shows detail of beading on the tongue of full beaded moccasin shown in color photo. Note the edging beading done in loops as shown in sketch.

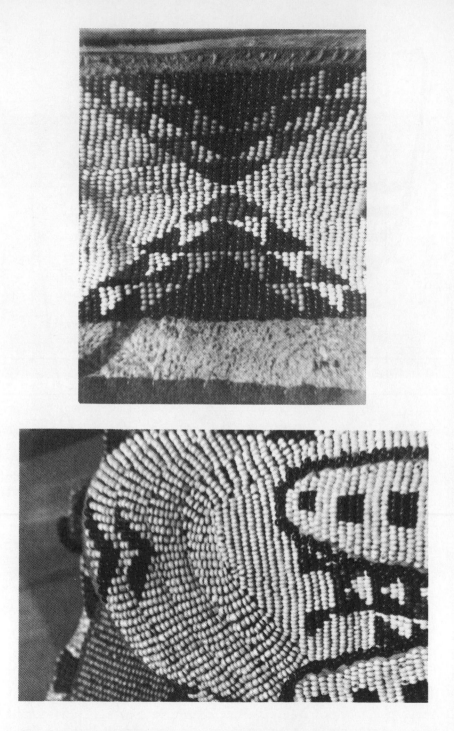

Top : Beading detail of the side of full beaded moccasin.

Bottom : Showing detail of toe. Note the changing of direction
in the rows of beads to better fit the contour of the toe.

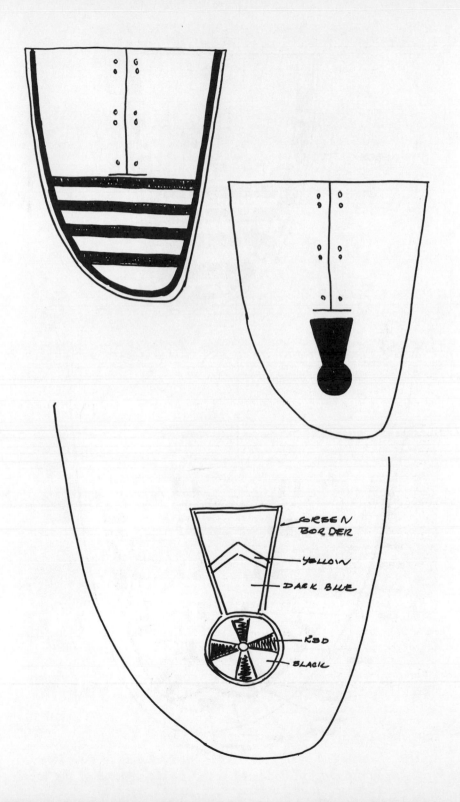

GREEN
BORDER

YELLOW

DARK BLUE

RED

BLACK

105

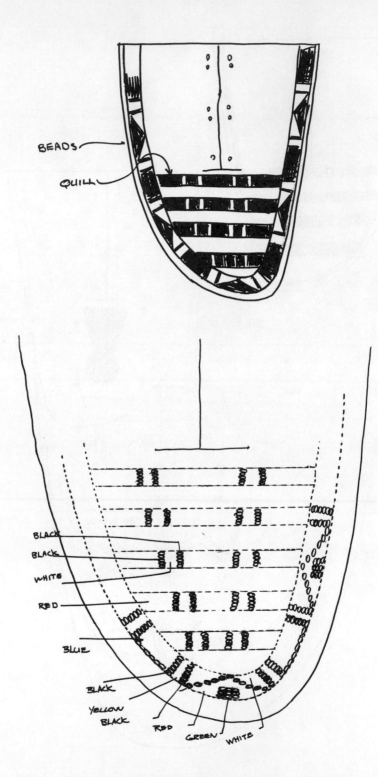

BEADS

QUILL

BLACK
BLACK
WHITE
RED

BLUE

BLACK
YELLOW
BLACK
RED
GREEN   WHITE

106

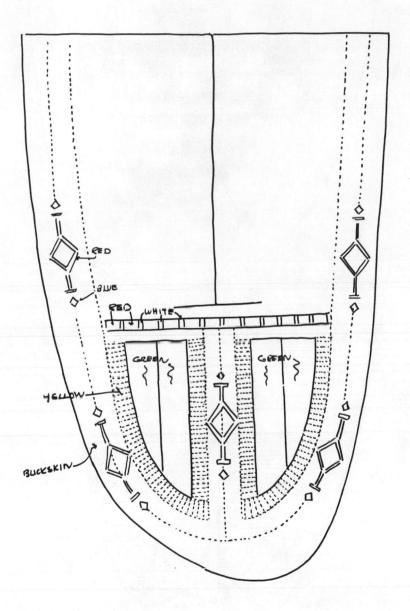

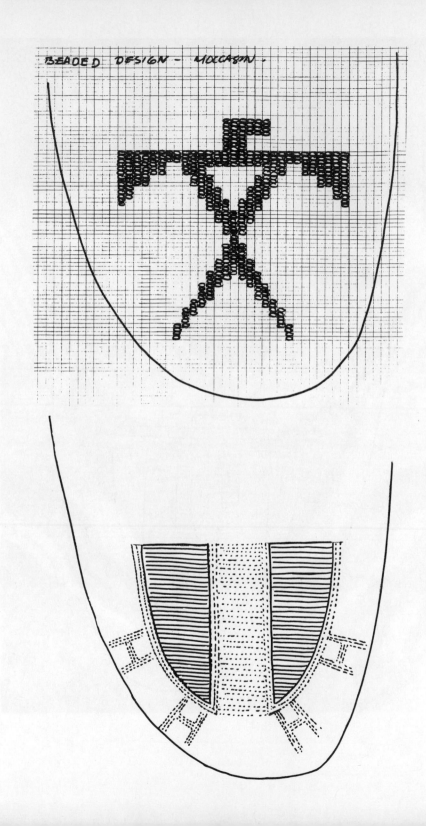

BEADED DESIGN - MOCCASIN.

These detail photos are of a moccasin which was among the things that Sally Anderson gave to Dr. White. Sally was the daughter of Reese Anderson, ranch foreman for Granville Stuart in central Montana. She salvaged the old 'junk' from her sister, who was cleaning out her cabin after high water had flooded the place. She told Sally how she had obtained the moccasins.

It seems a very wet and weary Indian rode to her cabin one fall day and asked for food. She gave him some bread and cold meat which he took to a haystack where he and the horse started dinner. Being cold and wet he sat in the sun and kicked off his moccasins. In the midst of the meal a clatter of shod hooves broke the stillness of the afternoon, as a group of soldiers jogged up to the cabin door. The Indian dropped everything, jumped on his pony and lit out, racing down the river bottom. Chances are the wet and tired troopers didn't relish the idea of swimming the river a second time and that they didn't see him again. Somehow, the old-time Indian could get extra mileage out of a horse.

Sallys' sister was attracted by the dogs finishing the lunch and discovered the moccasins. She took them in and hung them to dry, thinking he might return for them. Later she stored them with other things 'till many years later when flood waters had mildewed a trunkful of old Indian gear.

The beading on these moccasins shows a high sensitivity to color and the beading skill of a master craftsman.

110

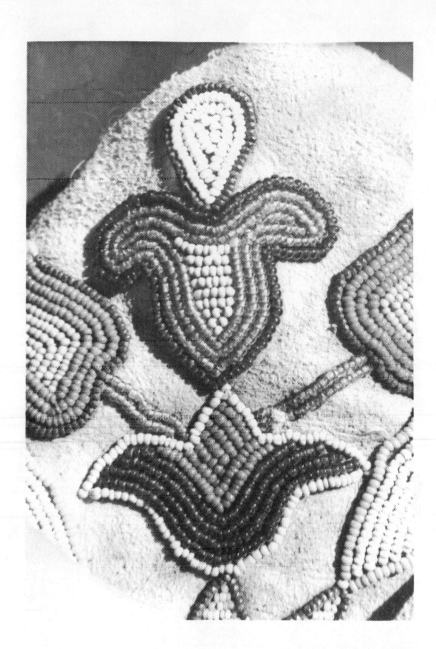

Detail photo showing full toe of moccasin on preceding pages.

Beading design of moccasins in photos. Probably Crow.

112

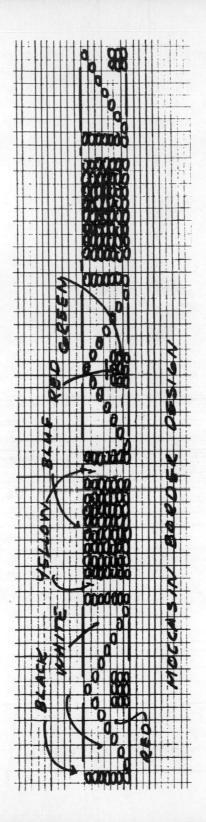

MOCCASIN BORDER DESIGN

113

Parfleche carrying cases, the 'Indian suitcase', provided large areas for decoration. Because of the texture of the parfleche (rawhide) it was unsuited for quill or bead work. Furthermore, its use was such that any decoration other than paint would be impractical. The designs which are found on these cases and other rawhide containers probably represent old traditional geometric designs.

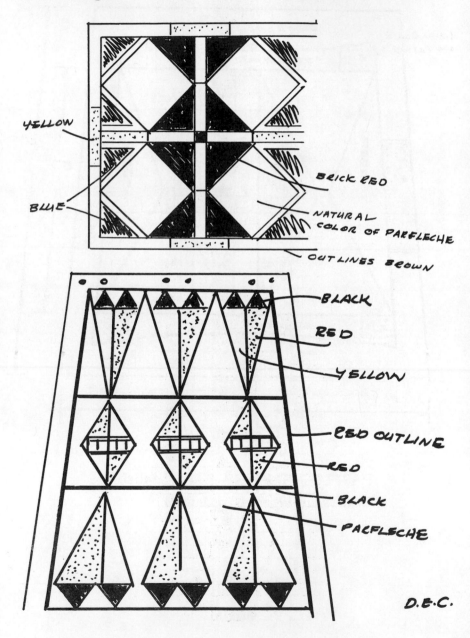

YELLOW

BLUE

BRICK RED

NATURAL COLOR OF PARFLECHE

OUTLINES BROWN

BLACK

RED

YELLOW

RED OUTLINE

RED

BLACK

PARFLECHE

114

D.E.C.

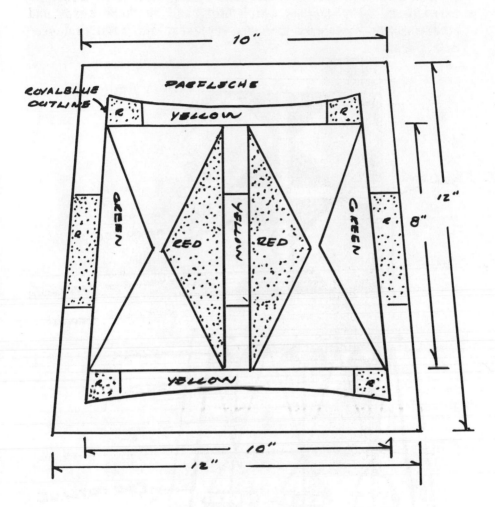

Figure labels: 10", 12", 8", PARFLECHE, ROYAL BLUE OUTLINE, R, YELLOW, GREEN, RED, YELLOW, GREEN, RED, R, R, R, R, YELLOW

PARFLECHE BERRY BAG (Salish)
Courtesy of Frances Vanderberg

Simple Quill Work - Wrapped around a pipe stem. The colors are *vermillion, purple, yellow, green and blue.* The wrapping and weaving of the quills had to be done at the same time, to get the rectangular colored areas properly placed.

The quill work ran the full length of the stem, with a ring of elk hair, bound by sinew, about midway down the stem.

Saddle maker Dick Ereaux and some of his collection. Note the endless variety of designs and uses of material.

117

DESIGNS SUITED FOR

LARGE HAND BAGS

AND OTHER LARGE SURFACES

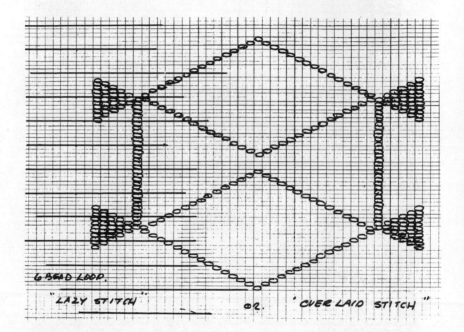

6 BEAD LOOP.

"LAZY STITCH"   OR.   "OVER LAID STITCH"

118

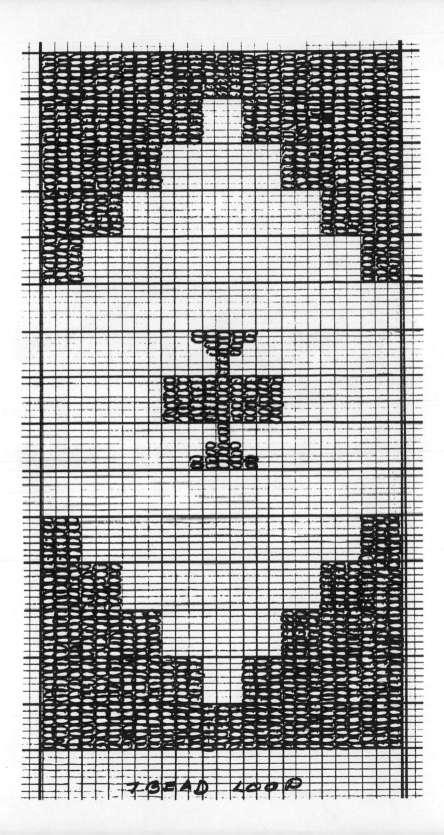

THREAD LOOP

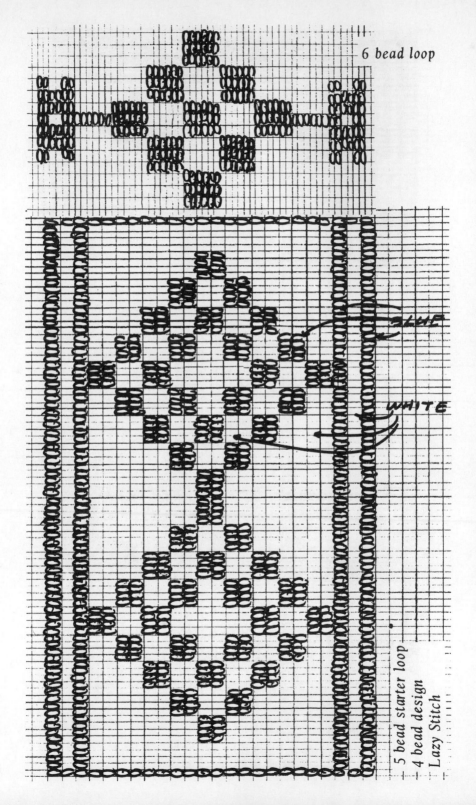

6 bead loop

BLUE

WHITE

5 bead starter loop
4 bead design
Lazy Stitch

120

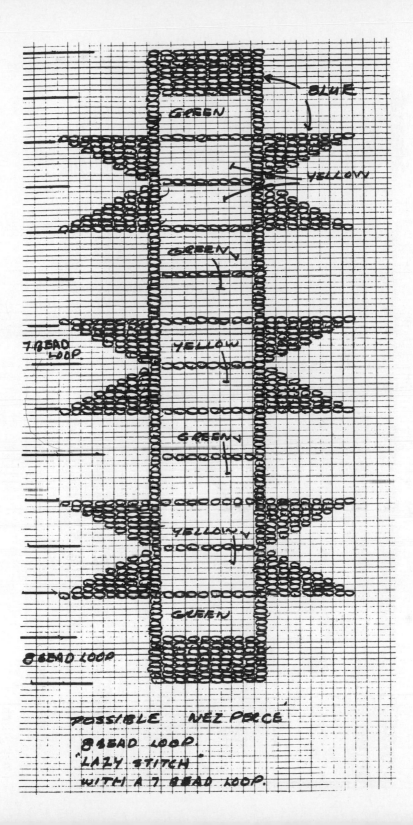

BLUE

GREEN

YELLOW

GREEN

7 BEAD
LOOP

YELLOW

GREEN

YELLOW

GREEN

8 BEAD LOOP

POSSIBLE NEZ PERCE
8 BEAD LOOP.
"LAZY STITCH"
WITH A 7 BEAD LOOP.

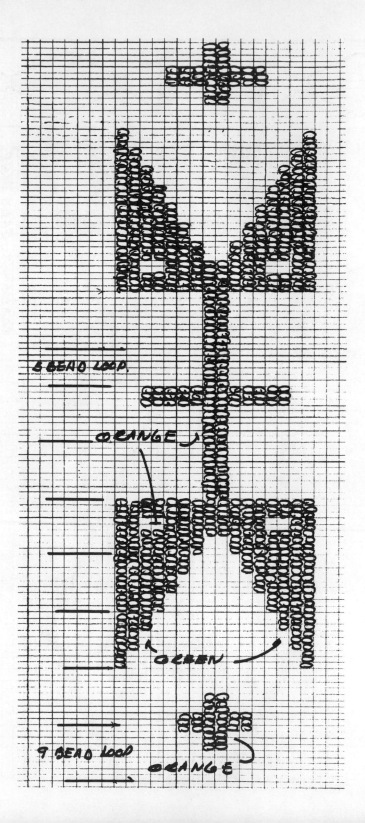

8 BEAD LOOP.

ORANGE

GREEN

122

9 BEAD LOOP

ORANGE

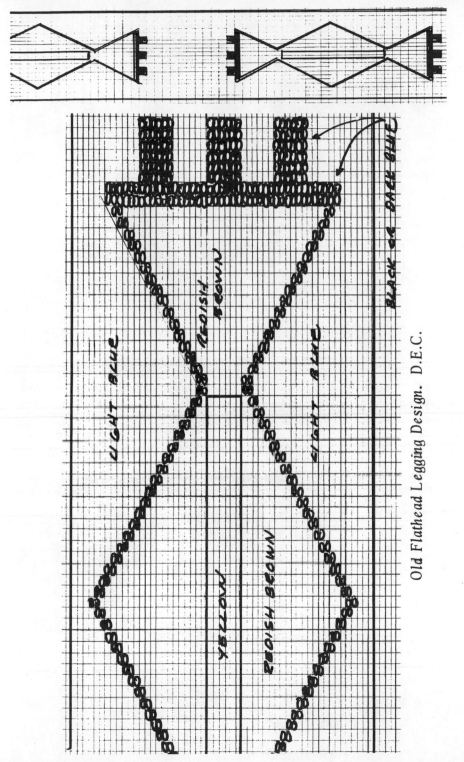

Old Flathead Legging Design. D.E.C.

123

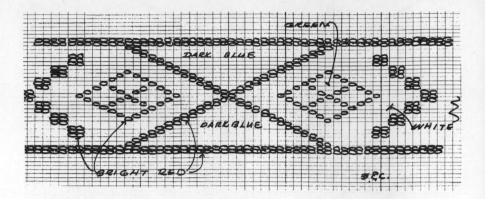

Within the beadwork diagram:
GREEN
DARK BLUE
DARK BLUE
WHITE
BRIGHT RED

CLOTH & BEAD CUFF
FLATHEAD LEGGING

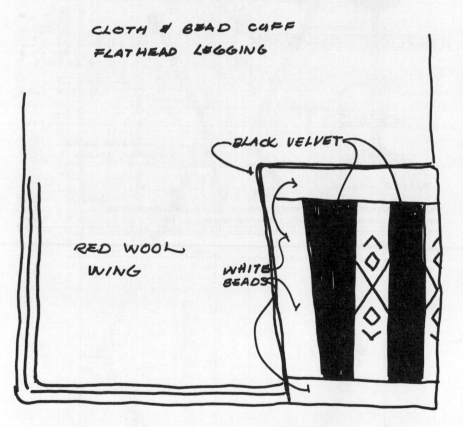

BLACK VELVET

RED WOOL
WING

WHITE
BEADS

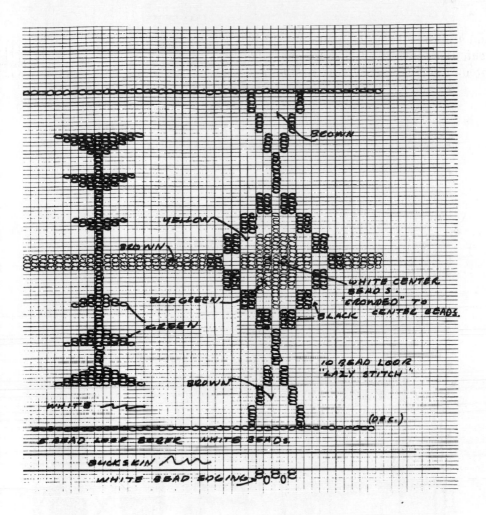

BROWN

YELLOW

BROWN

WHITE CENTER
BEADS.
"GROUNDED" TO
CENTER BEADS.

BLUE GREEN

BLACK

GREEN

10 BEAD LOOP
"LAZY STITCH"

BROWN

WHITE

(O.R.C.)

6 BEAD LOOP BIGGER WHITE BEADS.

BUCKSKIN

WHITE BEAD EDGING

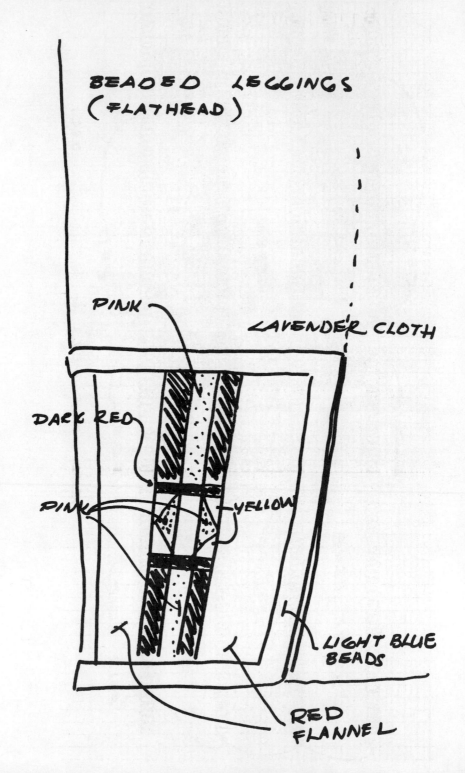

BEADED LEGGINGS
(FLATHEAD)

PINK

LAVENDER CLOTH

DARK RED

PINK

YELLOW

LIGHT BLUE BEADS

RED FLANNEL

126

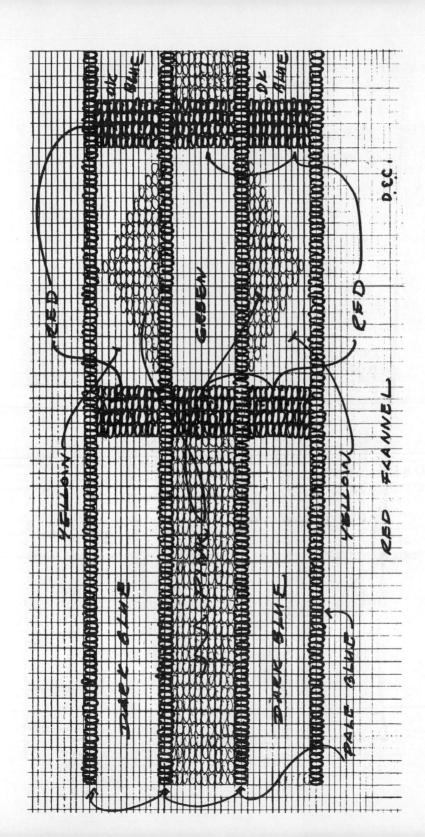

127

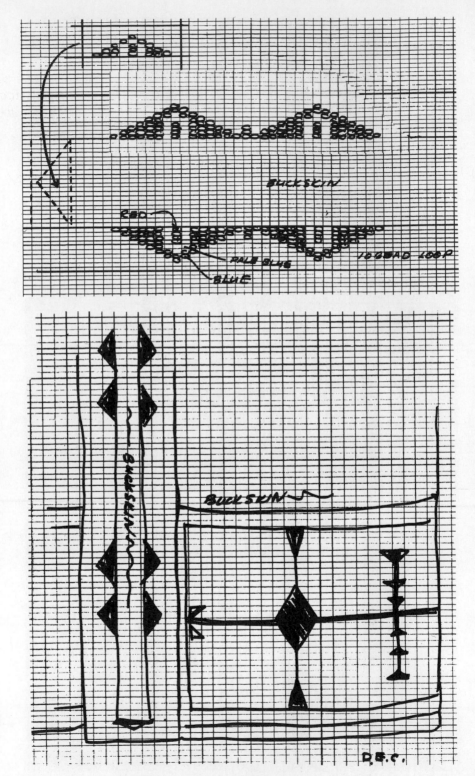

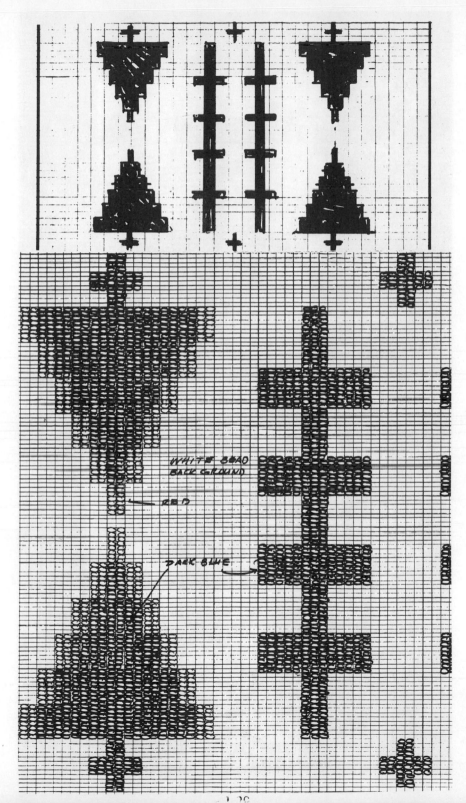

WHITE BEAD
BACK GROUND

RED

DARK BLUE

129

The miracle of birth was important to Indian people. Many kept the naval cord of the baby in a small pouch. With each year some object or bead was attached to the pouch. This may have been a personal history, or more significant, some spiritual function.

The pouch in the color photo to the left and detailed on the next several pages was a naval pouch of a member of the Ereaux family. It is probably Gros Ventre. D.E.C.

It displays some interesting beading techniques. One, the change of steps, (changes in design, vertical and horizontal) in this piece alternating between one step and two step to achieve the desired angle or slope of the design. The other point of interest is the 'crowding' done to the six end 'darts'.

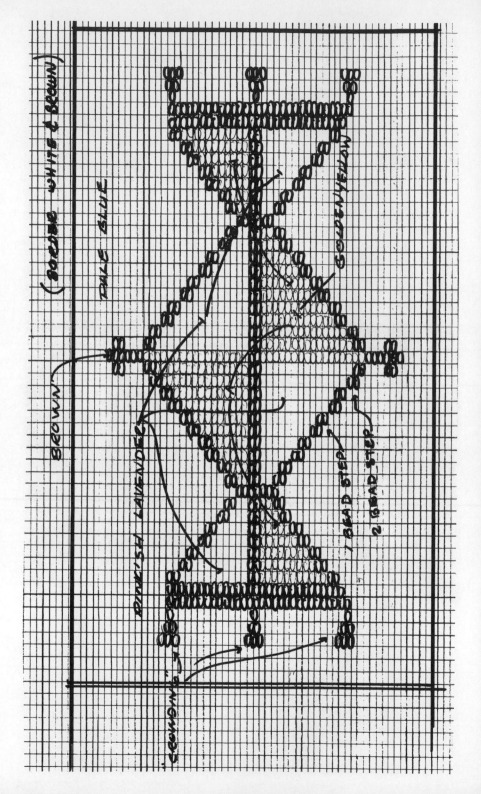

134

An interesting old Apache design. This design shows many variations in the pattern which would make it a good project for experienced beaders.

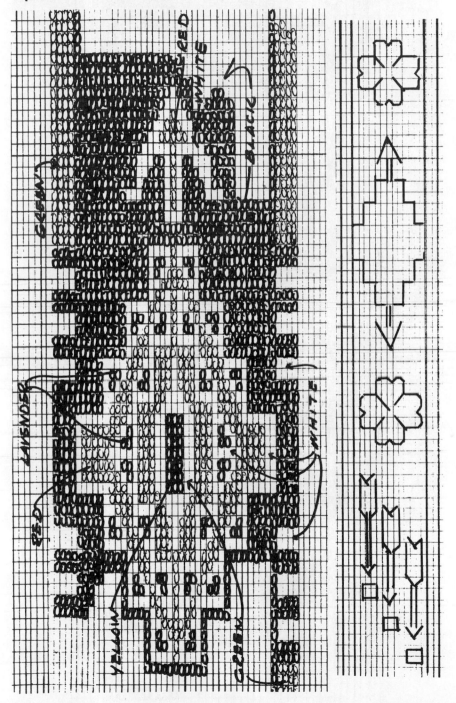

135

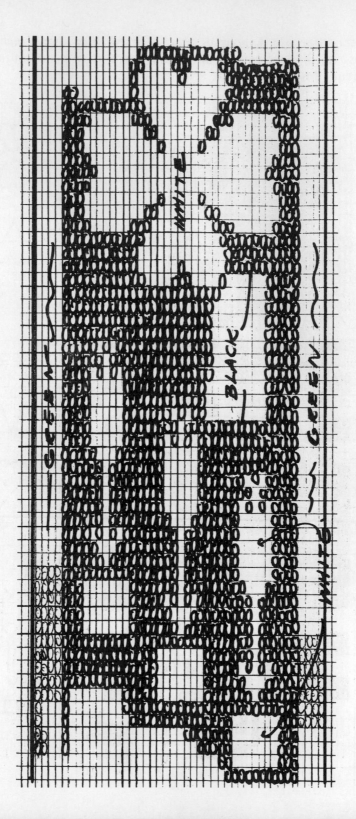

An old Pawnee legging design. Complex enough to challenge an experienced beader.

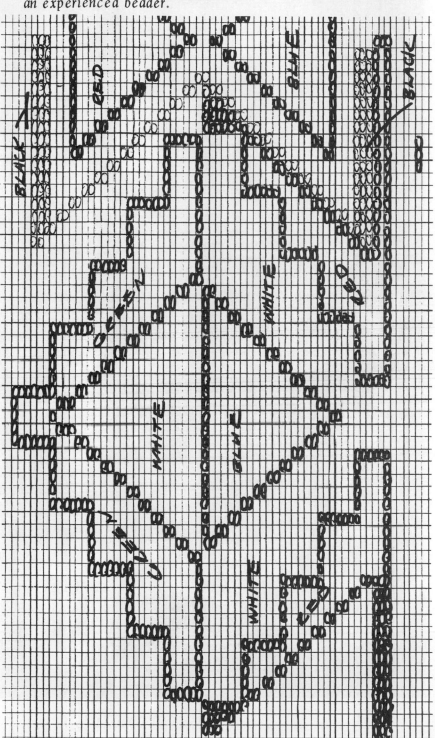

In the color photo to the left, the fringed bag is a Sioux tobacco pouch. This item shows a common use of quill and bead work in combination. Bead colors are somewhat typical of the Northern Plains Indians.

The long narrow item on the left is a Sioux quiver tab. Note the variance of bead sizes in center area, and also in areas of different color. The 'loops' may be eleven beads long or the bead size may change the count to ten or twelve beads. The length of the loop is more important than the bead count.

Old pieces often loosen or lose beads. This should not be confused with workmanship of the piece in its original state. The 'darts' at the bottom should be centered on the sixth bead of an eleven bead loop. However, 'artistic privilege' will allow other locations. (Refer to photo below)

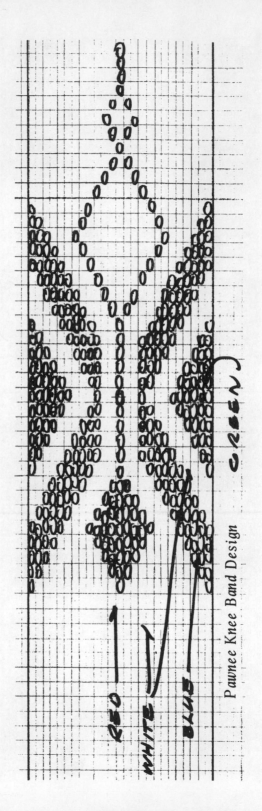

RED

WHITE

BLUE

GREEN

Pawnee Knee Band Design

140

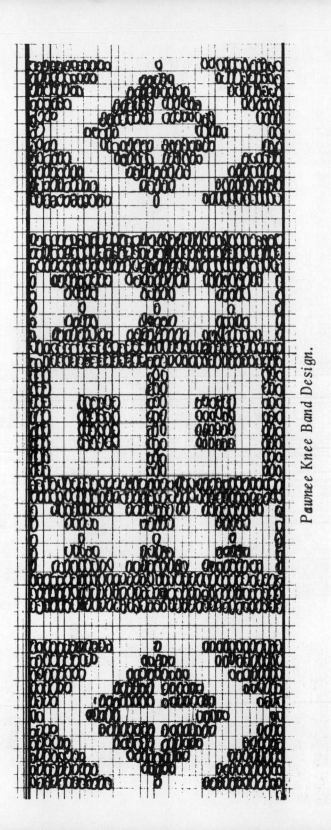

Pawnee Knee Band Design.

141

1865 Pawnee knee band design. The original band was about
three inches wide and was worn just below the knee.

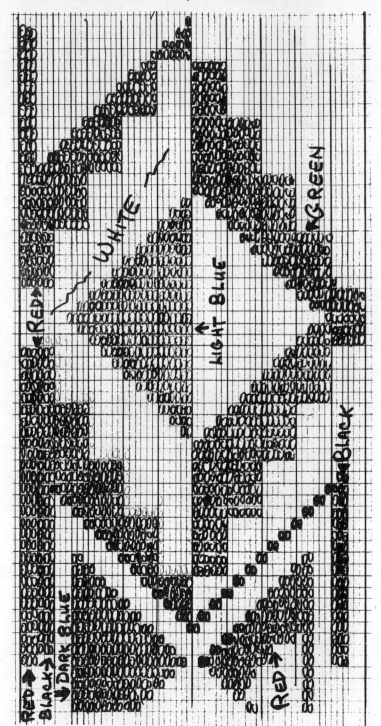

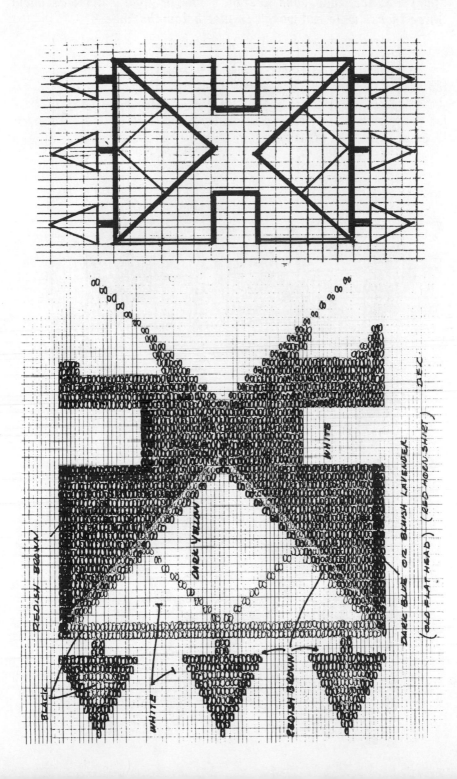

143

A hand bag (eight by ten inches) from the Dick Ereaux collection.   May be Flathead, but has Blackfoot characteristics.

A point of interest is the use of regular band construction for borders and the center portion is filled with beading parallel to band edge.   Beads on bag are tied at two or three bead intervals.

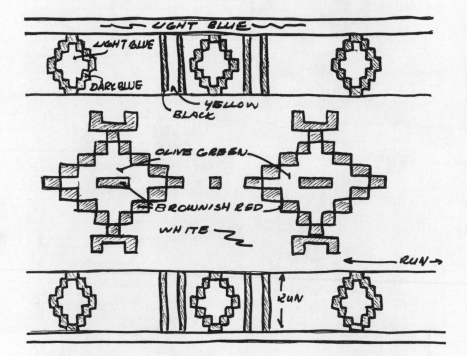

EXCELLENT   COLOR HARMONY -& WORKMANSHIP.
"OVERLAID STITCH" BEADS RUN IN TWO
DIRECTIONS

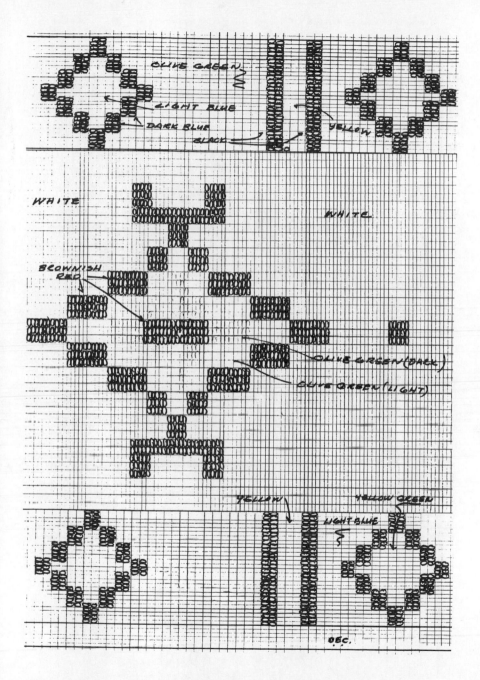

OLIVE GREEN

LIGHT BLUE

DARK BLUE

BLACK

YELLOW

WHITE

WHITE

BROWNISH RED

OLIVE GREEN (DARK)

OLIVE GREEN (LIGHT)

YELLOW

YELLOW GREEN

LIGHT BLUE

DEC.

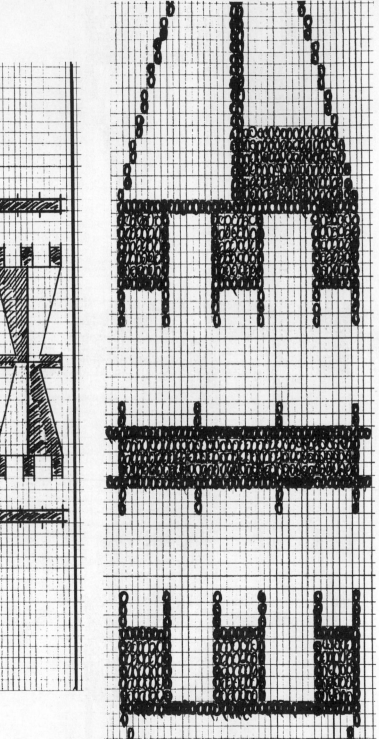

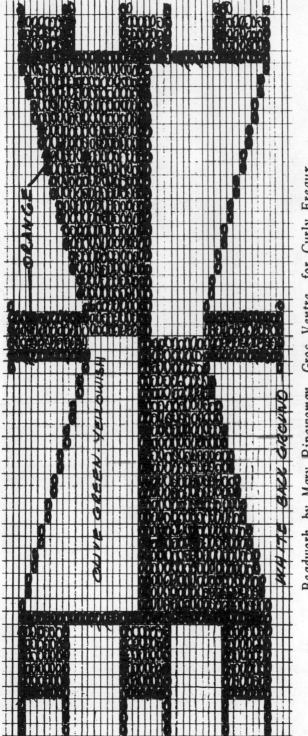

Beadwork by Mary Pipewoman, Gros Ventre, for Curly Ereaux,
early pioneer of Dodson, Montana. D.E.C.

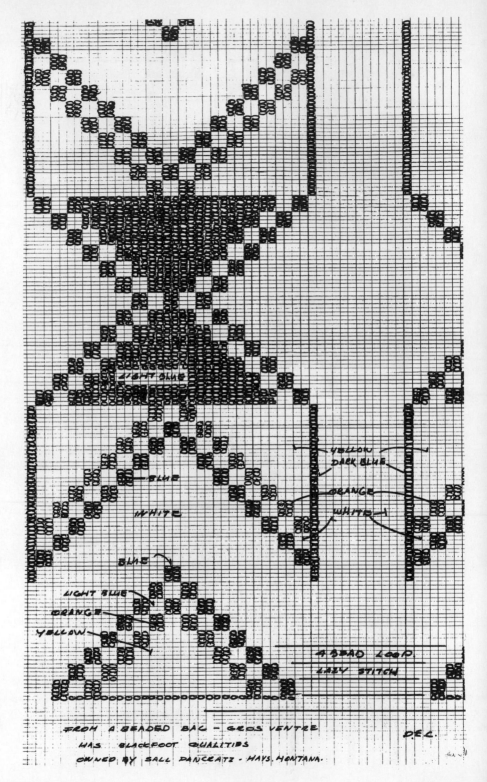

YELLOW
DARK BLUE

ORANGE

WHITE

LIGHT BLUE

BLUE

WHITE

BLUE

LIGHT BLUE

ORANGE

YELLOW

4 BEAD LOOP.

LAZY STITCH

FROM A BEADED BAG - GROS VENTRE
HAS BLACKFOOT QUALITIES
OWNED BY SALL DANCEATZ - HAYS, MONTANA.

D.E.C.

148

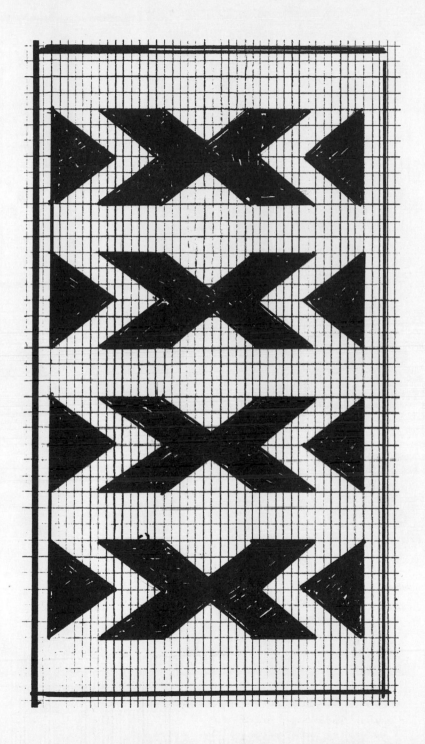

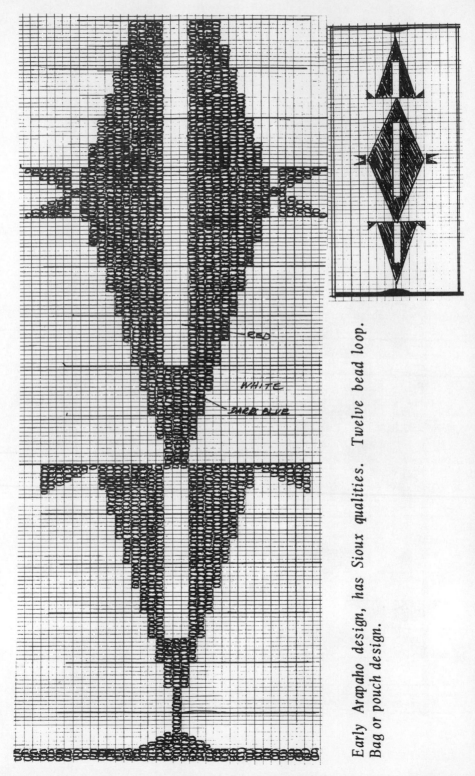

RED

WHITE

DARK BLUE

150

Early Arapaho design, has Sioux qualities. Twelve bead loop.
Bag or pouch design.

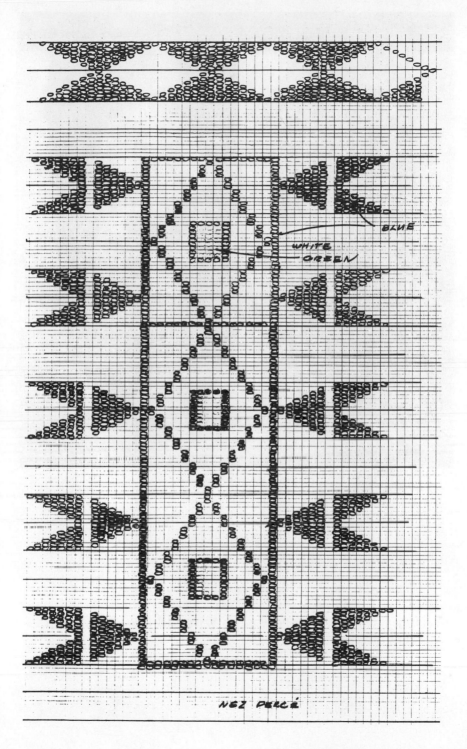

BLUE

WHITE
GREEN

NEZ PERCÉ

Left: Bandolier once owned by the Red Horn family. Very complicated, intricate beadwork. Various changes in design and bead color would suggest time intervals. This piece probably required many years to complete. D.E.C.

Right: Typical Flathead cradleboard, beaded on cloth over buckskin. D.E.C.

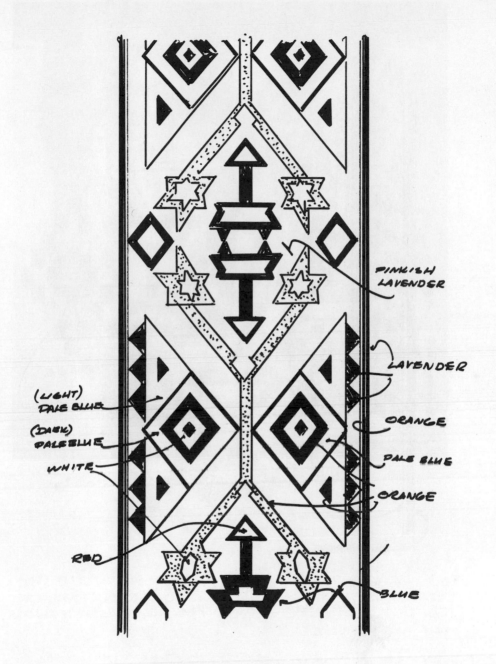

PINKISH LAVENDER

LAVENDER

(LIGHT) PALE BLUE

(DARK) PALE BLUE

WHITE

ORANGE

PALE BLUE

ORANGE

RED

BLUE

Shoulder band of bandolier.

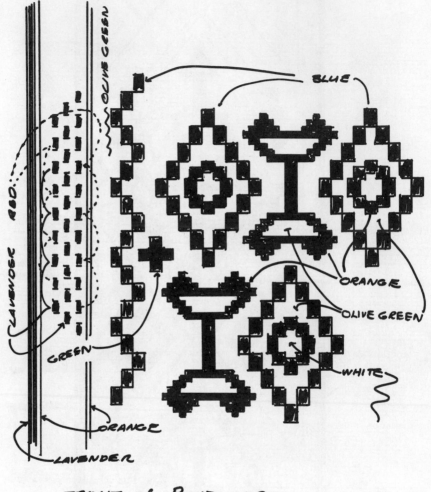

FRONT of BANDOLIER
(RED HORN FAMILY O.E.C.)

154

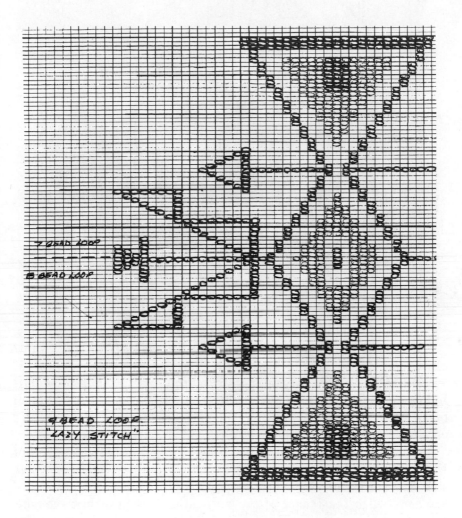

7 BEAD LOOP

13 BEAD LOOP

9 BEAD LOOP.
"LAZY STITCH"

155

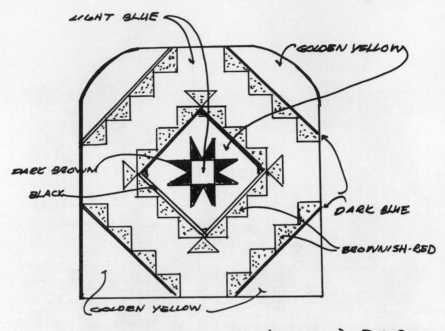

LIGHT BLUE

GOLDEN YELLOW

DARK BROWN

BLACK

DARK BLUE

BROWNISH-RED

GOLDEN YELLOW

EANIAS QUEQUESAH POUCH. (FLATHEAD) D.E.C.

This pouch belonged to Eanias Quequesah, Flathead. However, other pieces of the same technique appear to be Nez Perce.

This piece has several points of interest, such as the outlining of design areas, with double rows of beads, the filling of these areas and the 'crowding' in various spots. This piece is very well done and securely tied with the overlaid stitch.

Eanias's father, as a young man, walked with several other Flatheads to Hudson's Bay. It was a long journey, and the young man had some worry about seeing his home again. He expressed his concern to the leader of the party who looked at him thoughtfully for a moment. The leader then made a sign of the sun going from east to west and laid his left hand fingers across his right hand, which was to say: "just travel Southwest and you will get home."

This tale was told by Pete Beaverhead and interpreted by his wife Josephine.

Photo of beading of Eaneas Quequesah pouch.

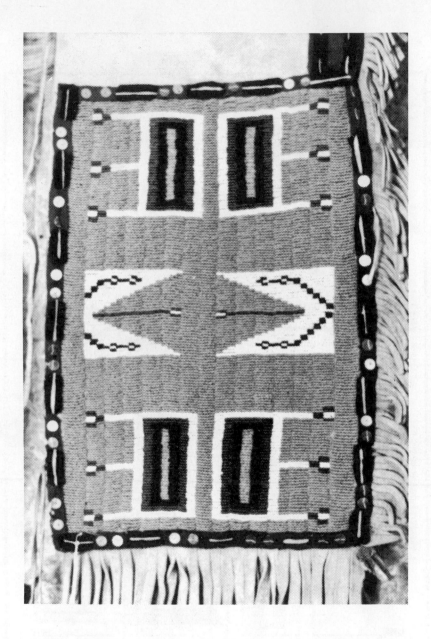

Old Crow saddle bag.   A beautiful piece of beadwork done in 'Lazy Stitch'.

Note the design change, center, left half.   An extra bar of 12 beads was added, forcing the white wings to the left and cutting off a 12 bead bar on the extreme left.

158

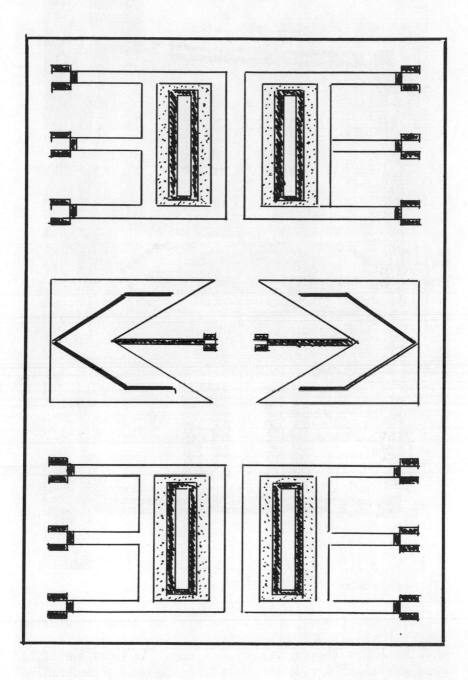

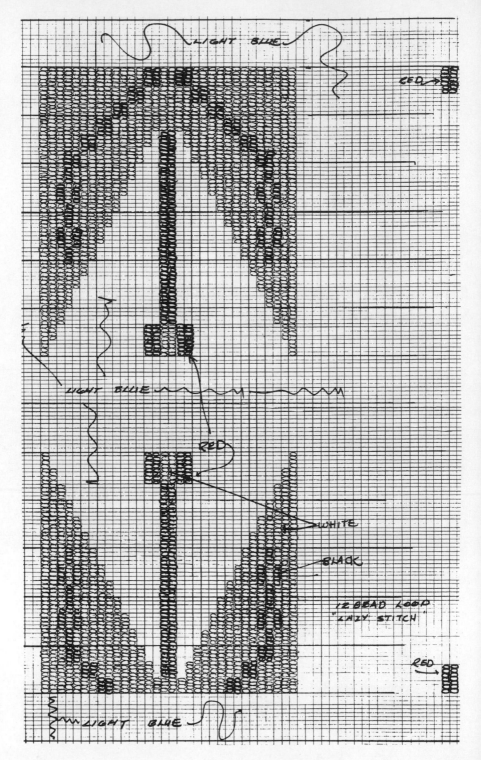

LIGHT BLUE

RED→

LIGHT BLUE

RED

WHITE

BLACK

12 BEAD LOOP
"LAZY STITCH"

RED

160

LIGHT BLUE

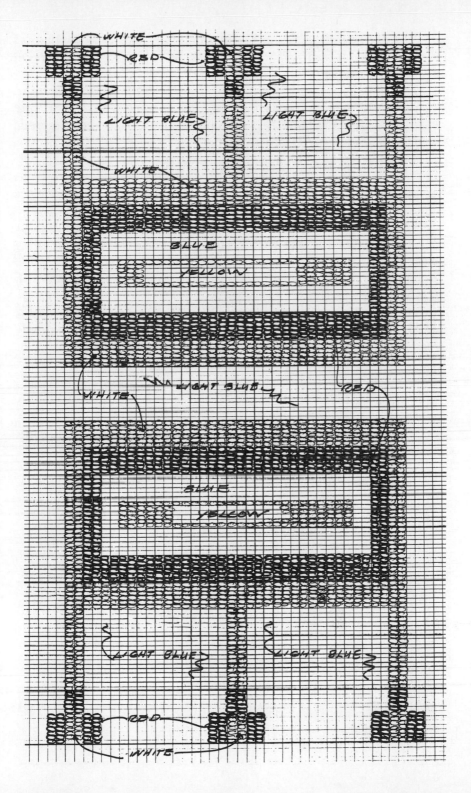

The possibility for different designs and combination of colors is almost endless. Those shown in this book represent only a small number of possibilities.

They do show proven designs of pleasing proportion and color. Changing the bead size will distort these proportions and care should be taken to retain these proportions (by altering the bead count in the rows) for maximum effect.

It would be well to note that the bead count as in loop patterns (Lazy Stitch) is not as important as the length of the loop. Variations in the bead size may require adding or subtracting a bead to produce the proper length.

On the Flathead Reservation a few women still tan their own hides using the old Indian method. Some is done for other people; some sold or traded; but most of it is converted into handcraft. They much prefer to bead good buckskin above all other material.

Most of the tanning is done in the Elmo area, as well as the majority of the beading. Other beaders are to be found, mainly around St. Ignatius, Ronan and Arlee.

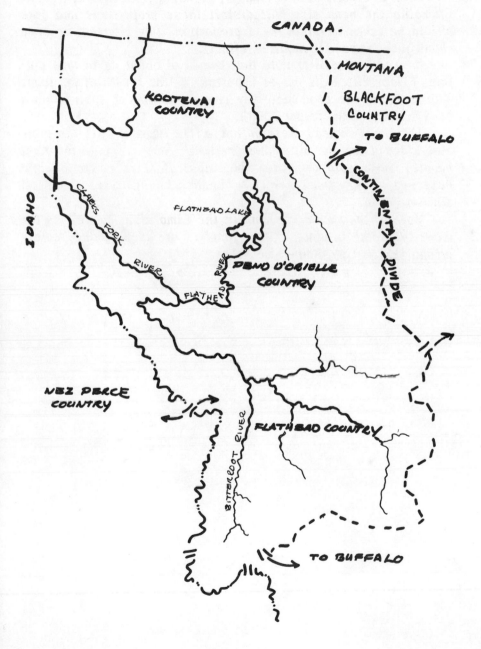

CANADA.

MONTANA

KOOTENAI COUNTRY

BLACKFOOT COUNTRY

TO BUFFALO

IDAHO

CLARKS FORK RIVER

FLATHEAD LAKE

PEND D'ORIELLE COUNTRY

FLATHEAD RIVER

CONTINENTAL DIVIDE

NEZ PERCE COUNTRY

BITTERROOT RIVER

FLATHEAD COUNTRY

TO BUFFALO